# PRAISE FOR POWER THINKING

"This is the wrong book for 85% of people. As Thomas Edison said, 'eighty-five percent would rather die than think.' Don Hooper shared his book with me at a critical time when I had some major challenges facing my company. I needed to change my mindset and try new models of thinking. Thank you, Don, for helping me see and think my way through these issues."
**—Jeff Patterson, Founder and CEO Gaggle.net**

"Don Hooper is on a scientific mission to help decision makers become mindful thought leaders through constructive problem solving and strategic, unbiased thinking. His new book, *Power Thinking: Discovering the Unknown by Unlocking Your Brain* provides the reader with a clear and practical combination of strong neuroscience as well as solid psychological guidance toward effective leadership. His Power Thinking models include tools to recognize, review, and analyze leadership challenges for identifying unknown possibilities in future planning."
**—Martha S. Burns, Ph.D, Director of Neuroscience Education, Carnegie Learning Corporation and Adjunct Faculty, Northwestern University**

"Thought leader, Don Hooper, Ph.D., provides a delicious recipe for creating intentionality around developing Power Thinking, the title of his new book. Dr. Hooper creatively and systematically puts together known thought practices that promote critical thinking while understanding brain science. He poses thought provoking questions that helps one understand the principles that projected innovators from Isaac Newton to Elon Musk.

Hooper provides a simple explanation of the brain power within each of us that, when exercised appropriately, can produce phenomenal life changing results. He says, 'Power Thinkers are problem solvers who use a combination of intuition and logical reasoning to come up with solutions while employing thinking skills to discover all aspects of a problem, while keeping in mind the difference in complex and simple thinking.' The thinking models introduced, although complex, provide a simple road map for achieving higher levels of thought complexity for anyone wishing to transform ordinary thought into extraordinary Power Thinking action!"
**—Mike Holt, Ph.D. Former Executive Director of School University Partnerships, Texas A&M University**

"Just like Napoleon Hill's blockbuster book *Think and Grow Rich*, Don Hooper's book *Power Thinking: Discovering the Unknown by Unlocking Your Brain* will impact thought leaders for decades to come. As a long time educator and leader, his approach to teaching others and his composition of neuroscience as an application to leadership and management makes this book a must read for elite thinkers. The tools he shares are powerful!"
**—Rod Paige, Former United States Secretary of Education**

"*Power Thinking* by Dr. Hooper gives you a snapshot of the valuable insights and lessons that Don acquired as a highly-respected superintendent and educational leader. This book is an important contribution for individuals wanting to review and improve their thinking models and skills. In the book, Don

provides specific strategic and tactical examples that you can begin using immediately to become a more effective problem solver and leader. Insights, wisdom, and lessons will resonate with readers seeking to improve their performance and upgrade their thinking skills. The book has already changed me."
**—Steve Miller, Ph.D., CEO and President Elite Performance Solutions**

"*Power Thinking* is essential when an investor or developer is considering a project that will be beneficial to all concerned. Don Hooper's book on Power Thinking opened my mind further to exercise different thinking strategies, thinking models, and deep-thinking practices to minimize risks and maximize opportunities for success. I have been in real estate for decades and this book helped me create a Masterpiece of Thought for development. Open your brain and cross the finish line."
**—John Femrite, Real Estate Investor**

# POWER THINKING

DISCOVERING THE UNKNOWN BY UNLOCKING
YOUR BRAIN

DON HOOPER, PH.D., CTL

— SOUL —
EXCELLENCE
PUBLISHING

Print ISBN: 979-8-9856016-7-1

Ebook ISBN: 979-8-9856016-6-4

# CONTENTS

# PROLOGUE

From the beginning of time, humans have been gifted with the ability to think, reason, feel emotion, desire, imagine, create ideas, try and fail, try and succeed, and persist or give up. What did those whom we recognize as having accomplished a great deal do the same or different from everyone else? Why?

When Albert Einstein, Thomas Edison, Plato, Socrates, Harriet Tubman, Katherine Johnson, Steve Jobs, Elon Musk, Jeff Bezos, Oprah Winfrey, Warren Buffett, Grant Cardone, and many others were born, did they not go through infancy, childhood, adolescence, and adulthood just like almost all humans? What set them apart? Was it riches, poverty, education, geography, historical times, race, gender, opportunity, or something else?

Sir Isaac Newton, when asked how he discovered gravity, said it was by thinking about what he was observing to the point of obsession. Yes, there is the classic "falling apple" story while drinking a cup of tea under an apple tree, but his obsession to think deeply and frequently using mental models as he observed the forces of nature gave him the courage to say to his peers that there is a "law of gravity." He employed observation, thinking, analysis, and the scientific method. Therefore, he discovered the then-unknown laws of gravity and motion and invented calculus (the mathematical study of continuous change). His "power thinking" helped to shape our rational worldview. Because Newton had been thinking about it all the time, when the apple fell, his mind was ready to notice and apply. Consider your future self: don't you want to be like Newton so that your Power Thinking will shape and impact our world for generations to come?

W. Clement Stone was a businessman, philanthropist, and *New Thought* self-help book author who is quoted as saying, "Whatever the mind of man can conceive and believe, it can achieve with PMA a positive mental attitude."[1] How will you use your mind?

You control your thoughts and attitudes. By learning Power Thinking, you will no doubt discover many unknown imaginations, ideas, creations, philosophies, inventions, systems, and much more to shape the future for a better you, which in turn shapes a better world.

Thought leaders are **Power Thinkers** who use the power of their mind and experience a transformation to elite thinking and can accomplish anything they desire if they conceive it, believe it, and achieve it.

Are you ready to engage your power?

Think of all the problems you will solve through Power Thinking. Think of the power of knowing exactly what you want and how to accomplish it. How powerful is finding your true purpose? How exciting will it be when you learn how to exercise your will to achieve what you want most? Let's begin to understand how the brain works so you can apply thinking skills at will and at the speed of thought!

# 1

# BRAIN BASICS: UNDERSTANDING THE SEAT OF THOUGHT

*Thought breeds thought; children familiar with great thoughts take as naturally to thinking for themselves as the well-nourished body takes to growing; and we must bear in mind that growth, physical, intellectual, moral, spiritual, is the sole end of education.*

— CHARLOTTE MASON, BRITISH EDUCATOR

S ince this book is about Power Thinking and since thinking occurs in the brain, it is helpful to first understand some of what modern science has discovered regarding the structure and function of the brain. The following is meant to provide a level of understanding of this most important part of our body and how we can direct it through our thoughts to yield our desired results.

But before we do that, I heard a story about a young man

who approached Socrates with a request. Socrates asked him what he wanted, and he said knowledge. Socrates took him to a river and held him underwater for ten seconds. He then let the young man up and asked him what he wanted. The young man repeated that he wanted knowledge. So, Socrates held him under water again only this time for twenty seconds before letting him up. Again, Socrates asked the question of what he wanted, and he again said knowledge. One more time, Socrates held him underwater only this time he waited until the young man struggled and flailed his arm before letting him up. Socrates then asked him what he wanted, and the young man shouted, "Air!" Socrates then told him that when he wanted knowledge as much as he wanted air, he would find it.

The Socratic method uses questions to understand values, principles, and beliefs to determine consistency with other beliefs. No doubt neuroscientists and others used the Socratic method to discover the unknown by employing such a technique. This book is about thinking, which is how the mind uses the brain to discover, learn, and explore with curiosity things that are new and exciting. As is the case with any item that is employed in an endeavor, the more the user knows about it, the more efficient and effective the user can get results that he or she desires. A Power Thinker wants to know how the brain works so that it can be used at a level that most people do not understand. So, bear with me as we explore what has been discovered about the brain so far.

**Anatomy of the Brain**

The brain is the control center of the body. The brain functions on chemicals and electrical impulses. That is why you may be aware that you can rewire your brain. There are neural pathways that are continually developing or are being used by your brain as you think about things. These have been developing in you since birth and interaction with others. You have power over your brain. Even a child knows what he or she wants before language is mastered. While this comes naturally, you can learn how to use that power at will.

## Brain Basics

The brain is the control center of the body. The brain has a wide range of responsibilities from coordinating our movement to managing our emotions. The brain is composed of three main divisions: the forebrain, brainstem, and hindbrain.

There are three main parts of the brain. The cerebrum is the most significant part of the brain and is where thoughts are processed, and memory may be stored. The cerebellum is located under the cerebrum and is at the brain's rear. This portion of the brain helps us maintain balance and equilibrium. It is also helpful in speech and coordination. Finally, the brain stem is connected to the spinal cord and helps regulate the body's automatic functions.

The brain also has hemispheres, lobes, and regions. The hemispheres are the left and right hemispheres, and each hemisphere has certain different functions and occasionally the same process.

According to the Mayfield Clinic, a neurosurgical clinic, the cerebrum is where reasoning occurs, and the left hemisphere is primarily responsible for controlling speech, comprehension, arithmetic, and writing. In other words, the left hemisphere is the logical and reasoning hemisphere. The right hemisphere controls creativity, spatial ability, and artistic and musical skills. The two hemispheres are connected by what is known as the corpus callosum. The corpus callosum is a large bundle of more than 200 million myelinated nerve fibers that connect the two brain hemispheres, permitting communication between the right and left sides of the brain. The corpus callosum consists of the nerve fibers that connect the brain hemispheres and facilitate communication between the hemispheres. Later, when we mention Executive Stewardship and whole-brain activity, it is essential to realize that by conscious thought, we can use all parts of our brain to capitalize on the particular specialty of each area.

In addition to hemispheres, the brain also has lobes. There are four main lobes. First, problem-solving occurs primarily in the frontal lobe. The parietal lobe primarily interprets signals from vision, hearing, motor, sensory impulses, and memory; the occipital lobes primarily interpret our vision; finally, the temporal lobe understands language, memory, hearing, sequencing, and organization.

As one can see, the brain is very intricate and exciting in form, function, and utility.

There is so much to learn about the brain and how it affects our lives, our ability to imagine, invent, innovate, relate, control actions, avoid disaster, and create.

## Neurochemistry

There are happy chemicals in your brain. Dopamine (immediate pleasure), serotonin (mood regulation and memory), oxytocin (social bonding, motivationally relevant stimuli), and endorphins (natural pain and stress chemicals released by the pituitary gland) make up the happy chemicals. These reward you when you do something that contributes to thriving and to your survival which amounts to thriving while surviving or as I call it your "thrival" of accomplishing things you want to do. The job of the unhappy chemical, cortisol, is to warn you of danger. The neural pathways carry the brain chemicals. These can be used and new ones built if you know how. Neurons are the elements, and neural pathways are the highways that connect them. Your brain meets its need to find more of what is happy and avoids what is a threat or remembering an unhappy experience.

Electricity flows through the neural pathways. Feed the brain new experiences, and you create new neural pathways to create new habits. This leads to the development of either a positive or a negative mental attitude. How you view your survival also depends upon your mind's eye of what you want to accomplish. Some people refer to this as a mindset. Carol Dwek in her book on mindsets says there are two basic mindsets, fixed or growth. You can set your mind to accomplish something in a way that makes you happy, so your brain releases the happy chemical cocktail to keep you with that mindset that makes you happy. Some people are happy with a fixed mindset for certain things and a growth mindset for other things. You have the power to control your thoughts. Dopamine is released when you view something in your mind's eye that you want to do and believe that you can accomplish it. This stops when you accomplish it. That is why some people say the journey is more fun than the destination. That is why you must do more to get more. This also creates a neural pathway that paves the way for the happy journey to be replicated.

Your mind's eye can change lenses much like a camera. What lens do you choose? In other words, what do you want to focus your thoughts on? Warren Buffet, a famous investor and billionaire, has an investor's eye. Always examining market data and making intuitive decisions based on thought and experience combined with creativity to make great investments. Another billionaire is Bill Gates, founder of Microsoft corporation, and he has a technologist's eye. Sparring with different minds' eyes allows you to see things differently. This synergy results in an incredible mind meld, which enriches your thinking. In a way, your mind's eye is a thinking model that changes as your focus changes. To see mentally is to think.

Distraction changes the flow of your brain electricity along one neural pathway to another, and with that, a brain chemical is released. Distractions can be important or unimportant, and one can manage distractions based upon experience and commitment. Interruptions happen frequently. Some are given attention, and others are ignored or placed secondary in importance. Some interruptions happen with such magnitude that they become disruptions, which change the course of action and accomplishment.

New pathways or wiring in the brain are due to the repetition of thought. You can create a new habit of thought. Consider adopting the following four-step rewiring plan:

- **Step 1:** choose a specific thought that you want to use as a trigger for the new path each time that thought occurs.
- **Step 2:** select the proper opportunity to trigger the thought.
- **Step 3:** make energy available for this project as you commit to it, and be consistent in the thinking of the new thought.
- **Step 4:** continue to strengthen the new pathway

We can build a new dopamine pathway by selecting new short-, medium-, and long-term goals. We can build a new oxytocin pathway by interacting with others in a meaningful way with small steps by imagining the motivation or motive for action to complete a desired goal or accomplishment. Suppose you wanted to create a new social bonding group or join an existing group. When you do this, you feel a rush of serotonin. Serotonin is a neural chemical that helps with a feeling of closeness or belonging. Endorphins are built for emergencies, so no regular pathway is set for them. Laughter can trigger these endorphins even if it is contrived laughter. Look for healthy ways to stimulate the happy chemicals by developing happy habits.

Our brain's cognitive power—that is, our ability to learn, remember, and solve problems—slows down with age. Aging is a natural process. Even the most gifted athlete and performer lose their agility over time due to aging, but they are still, because of their physical and mental conditioning at an earlier age, more capable than individuals who have not performed at an elevated level. The dedication to skill and conditioning may diminish over time but still, be greater than that of an individual who has never trained at those levels. Many of us find it harder to remember once-familiar facts. These changes affect our ability to focus, so we may find ourselves getting more easily distracted than when we were younger. You may have noticed a common practice of playing word games or number games to increase or maintain cognitive abilities. Just like physical exercise is good for most of the body, mental exercise is good for our brain and its capabilities. These mental exercises performed while thinking can be referred to as a "thinkercise". We can do a "thinkercise" for a "thinkersize" result. By exercising our brain, we can increase our dreams and goals to a size we desire. Yes, it is a play on words, but perhaps we should be more creative in our thoughts. Our thought ability usually stays with us longer than our physical abilities. As we age, we may need a walker or eyeglasses or hearing aids, but many in their 90s or even at age 100 can still communicate and think even though their physical ability to move is restricted. Be sure to understand and take care of your mind. It should be with you even at an advanced age.

When we learn about the brain, we hear about neurons. A neuron's specific function is to help the brain, itself made up of billions of neurons, remember, learn, and reason. The body can react based on information sent and received by the neurons. When the body reacts, commands are sent from the brain to muscles and glands via neurons known as neurotransmitters which send a message across a synapse. So, without becoming a neuroscientist, let's dig a little deeper into how a neuron works.

## Neuron

We have both neurons and nerves. Neurons generate electrical and chemical signals; nerves provide an environment for conducting these signals. A nerve uses electrical and chemical signals to transmit sensory and motor information from one body part to another.

## Synapse

A synapse is a small gap structure that connects neurons as they send electrical or chemical signals to each other, responding to synaptic activity and, in turn, regulating neurotransmission.

Synapses connect with other nerve cells. Synapses are vital to the brain's function, especially when it comes to memory.

In the central nervous system, a synapse is a small gap at the end of a neuron that allows a signal to pass from one neuron to the next. Synapses are found where nerve cells connect with other nerve cells. Synapses are key to the brain's function, especially when it comes to memory.

The five senses (sight, hearing, touch, smell, taste) send electricity to your brain. Connected neurons create meaning. Consider your physical reaction to walking into your favorite eating establishment. You can see the menu and prepared food, smell the aroma, hear the hubbub of happy patrons, and want to taste the food of your choice. You may not realize that these sensations are sending signals to your brain where dopamine, oxytocin, and serotonin are being released. The anticipation of the experience is sensational. In your brain, previously established pathways are wired together and are firing together. Pathways make you who you are. As stated earlier, we can create a new pathway with our rewiring plan. It is simple to use, and once we learn how to do it, the fun begins. Past experiences are neurochemical activated and reactivated since they have created regular pathways to repeat action. However, you can create a new pathway. Past experience pathways enable one to process more with less effort on existing pathways, but new ones take energy. Conscious effort is needed to build a new pathway. The jump across a synapse to the receptor and continued practice make efficient connections and creates new pathways.

Whatever triggered the chemicals in the past will also trigger them now very quickly based upon the experience. When you feel good, the brain is releasing dopamine, oxytocin, and serotonin; when the brain senses danger, cortisol is released; and when the body needs relief from pain, endorphins are released. This explains what is known as the runner's high that enables determined long-distance runners to continue even though they may experience pain. I have a family member who trains for and runs marathons. The mental and physical training that is needed for these events is phenomenal. In visiting with him, an understanding of how the brain works is helpful for his physical and mental preparation and determination not only to complete a full marathon but also to set targets to improve his performance. Endorphins secrete when we see a survival need such as running a marathon or dealing with a physical emergency for survival. Social needs are essential to survival, so they are central to our happy chemicals. Remember, dopamine creates the feeling that a reward is at hand and a need is about to be met. That is a motivation to act. In other words, a motive for action. Additional triggers of dopamine occur each time the goal gets closer. When the goal is attained, the dopamine stops because it has already done its job. This is the brain signal that now is the time to go for it. Since energy is not without limits, survival is met with making careful decisions about which goals to reach. Neurons connect when dopamine flows and creates brain pathways and habits.

Is there an individual whom you know, like, and trust? Do they feel the same about you? It feels good, doesn't it? You might not realize it, but oxytocin creates a feeling of trust. While this is true, we make careful decisions to trust and have a personal close interaction and enjoy each other. The neural pathways of each such experience guide our decision for future interactions. We remember how it feels to hug or kiss a family member and to cuddle a grandchild so we want to do so more frequently. You want to repeat this action frequently in person, and the good feeling also happens in memory and in anticipation of seeing them and holding them again.

This feeling of trust is important when selecting a mastermind group to work with on a definite purpose. Individuals who are selected to become part of a mastermind group must be trustworthy and be like-minded about the purpose of that group. When the group meets, whether it is in person or remotely, purpose, vision, mission, goals, strategies, and tactics will be discussed. As this happens, brain chemicals will be triggered in each participant. Dopamine leads you to go for a goal, oxytocin leads you back to the mastermind. Serotonin creates the great feeling of social importance and peace. This is emitted when you see yourself in a strong position of success, especially when your success is recognized by your mastermind group or others outside your group. We love to be part of a group because of this. Whether the group is a family, a sports team, a gaming group, or a mastermind group, the neural pathways in each participant's brain are established and become part of the culture of that group.

Our world is volatile, uncertain, chaotic, and ambiguous (VUCA). That is why we can learn to orient our viewpoint, observe our current situation, decide upon a new course of action, and act on the new course (OODA Loop). Cortisol, the stress chemical, is released when you see yourself in a weaker position or when danger threatens. Setting a new action can release dopamine, which motivates you to escape the danger and return to safety. When we mention that we live in a VUCA world and employ the OODA Loop, we learn how to control our brain chemical secretions since we are in control of our thoughts. Cortisol will be the main chemical release unless we change our thoughts to deal with the new threat in a separate way. This helps us mitigate the cortisol release that brings on stress. Stress is not always a terrible thing if it is managed properly. Learning how to breathe to oxygenate the brain for clear thinking will help us recognize what is happening so we can think about it and act to remove or avoid the stressor. This process will allow us to set a new goal, which can counteract the cortisol with dopamine release since we have set a new expectation rather than the one we originally faced. All of this is thought power. Power Thinkers exercise thought power. The breathing is equally important to the thinking.

Applied faith is believing something can be done and then acting accordingly. Thinking must precede faith since we can only develop faith by thinking about what to believe. Once we believe in something, it is easier to apply that faith by employing action that, when sustained with positive thoughts, triggers dopamine rather than letting dangerous or negative thoughts trigger cortisol. Serotonin can be triggered in such a way that you must do more to get more, especially when cortisol is triggered. Cortisol is also triggered by disappointment, such as when expectations of success are disappointed. This affects moods and depression. Threats are both internal and external. Our internal threats are our negative thoughts. Cortisol stays in your body longer than happy chemicals, so persistence of thought is especially important to a positive or negative attitude. Cortisol is secreted shortly in a stressful situation and continues to secrete until the stressful situation is controlled or a new thought process leads to a new experience. Distraction or taking a break is important to change the cortisol release because you can direct your thoughts to something else to help with shortening the existence of cortisol. A couple of hours of distraction lets the body metabolize the cortisol while you are distracted. This helps remove the brain fog that can develop or the sense of hopelessness or regret from not acting differently. Threatened feelings do not make for good decision-making; that is why a break is needed. Old pathways are powerful. However, they can be left behind while new pathways are established and maintained.

Any thinker, especially a Power Thinker, can and will choose a new behavior or thought pattern that will serve him or her well. When one repeats the new choice, the synapses often become efficient and then boost that electricity by spending less energy on other things. This is how new neural pathways are created and new habits are formed.

## Neuroplasticity

Neuroplasticity is the ability of neural networks in the brain to change through growth and reorganization. It is the brain's ability to continue growing and evolving in response to life experiences throughout our lives regardless of age. It is the ability of neural networks in the brain to change through growth and reorganization. We can use our brain to form and reorganize synaptic connections, especially in response to learning or experience following an injury or stimuli based upon a physical stimulus or a thought stimulus. A thinker can spend time identifying current neural networks and decide to keep them or change them.

Our brain is a dynamic connected power grid of electrical impulses. There are billions of pathways lighting up every time you think, feel, or act. Some of these pathways are often traveled due to our habits or our established ways of thinking, feeling, or doing. Every time we think in a certain way, practice a particular task, or feel a specific emotion, we strengthen and widen the path to become a habit of thinking and makes the pathway one of least resistance. We can choose a new way of thinking, a new way of doing something, or a new emotion and thereby create a new neural pathway that will be strengthened with more repetition until this new pathway and this new way of thinking, doing, or feeling becomes second nature. The old pathway gets used less and less and atrophies. This process is how we rewire our brain at will as we choose by forming new connections and weakening old ones. This is neuroplasticity in action. In other words, we all possess the ability to learn and change by rewiring our brains regardless of our age.

The prefrontal cortex is critical for things like decision-making, focus, attention, and personality. It has right and left temporal lobes of the brain and engages the deep limbic system to form and keep long-term memory. This is the hippocampus. The hippocampus is the region of the brain that is associated primarily with memory, both short and long. The hippocampus creates memory by the encoding, storage, and retrieval in the human mind of past experiences. Every one of us wants a "Happy Hippo" since it is key to our wellbeing and memory.

Learning could not occur without the function of memory. So-called intelligent behavior demands memory, remembering being the prerequisite to reasoning. The ability to solve any problem or even to recognize that a problem exists depends on memory. Routine action, such as the decision to cross a street, is based on remembering numerous earlier experiences. The act of remembering an experience and bringing it to consciousness later requires an association, which is formed from the experience, and a "retrieval cue," which elicits the memory of the experience. This happens when the amygdala is in a happy state and relaxes the hippocampus to access the store of memory.

Practice (or review) tends to build and maintain memory for a task or for any learned material. During a period without practice, what has been learned tends to be forgotten. Although the adaptive value of forgetting may not be obvious, dramatic instances of sudden forgetting (as in amnesia) can be seen to be adaptive. Indeed, when one's memory of an emotionally painful experience leads to severe anxiety, forgetting may produce relief. The functions of the hippocampus are associated with feeling and reacting. The hippocampus plays a key role in the limbic system, which is situated on the edge of the cortex and includes the amygdala and hypothalamus. These structures aid in controlling the different body functions, such as the endocrine system and memory, and regulating emotions. They belong to the limbic system and play major roles in long-term memory and spatial navigation. Now that you recognize this, you can focus on happy thoughts to relieve stress, open up your memory pathways, and be creative.

The hippocampus is a central structure within the brain, responsible for handling the storage of memories and the linking of memories to sensations. Another function of the hippocampus is aiding in navigation by enabling spatial memory. There are two hippocampi in the brain, one in each cerebral hemisphere. When stress or fear is triggered through the amygdala, the hippocampi shrink, and learning is more difficult. When happiness and wellbeing are triggered in the amygdala, the hippocampi open and function more in our favor to accomplish what we genuinely want to accomplish.

Exercise is the most important thing you can do for your brain. By doing a single workout, your body increases neurotransmitters like dopamine, serotonin, and noradrenalin, which increases your reaction time and mood and gives you the ability to shift and focus your attention. It also provides needed oxygen to the brain for peak performance.

Since each person is different, there is not a set length of time the neural chemicals stay active. The entire brain and the function of the brain is changed by exercise. Exercise creates new brain cells. In the hippocampus, exercise increases its size and its volume of secretions, which improves your long-term memory. Exercise also increases your ability to concentrate, which helps activate the prefrontal cortex. Focus and attention are important and occur when the hippocampus is expanded by a feeling of wellbeing. Physical exercise also strengthens both the mind and the body.

Neurons, when connected, convey meaning. That is why repetition is needed to form a new habit. It is true the brain stem can hear all sounds even before a person is born. But depending upon where geographically a person is reared as a child the language and accent that is spoken is the one the brain develops, and the other sound abilities are atrophied. So, regardless of ethnicity, the geographic location and the language sounds heard as a child are the one the brain holds on to. This explains accents in speech even into a new language environment.

Brain plasticity (neuroplasticity) is the most pliable before the age of puberty, but brain plasticity exists throughout our entire life regardless of age. The language you learned as a child with its accents is your dominant accent due to synaptic pruning. However, depending upon the individual ability to listen to sounds some persons can speak many languages imitating the accents of that home language location. The "use it or lose it" principle is activated. So, use of every aspect of the brain preserves its pliability, and failure to use a part of the brain ends the original neural pathways.

When restoring the brain, scientists focus on new neural pathway building rather than just trying to reconnect an existing pathway. Synapses that are often used have strong connections. While the rarely used synapses are eliminated due to synaptic pruning. This makes the brain more efficient since energy is no longer provided to the unused connections. Development of new neural pathways is where learning occurs. We can become life-long learners if we are willing to exercise this amazing gift of power. Brain plasticity is what allows new neuro brain pathways to form and new habits to be formed. Modern science has now proved that brain plasticity lasts even into old age.

When you remember past experiences or think about repeating them, the same brain chemicals that are associated with those memories are released. Therefore, by controlling your thoughts, you also control the chemical releases in your brain for either good purposes or bad purposes. You can build new pathways with conscious effort. This is where you exercise the power of will or volition, and since consistency compounds, you can develop an extraordinarily strong willpower. This takes effort initially but becomes easier over time because of persistent focused effort. Decide a course of action, put all your energy into that, and persist in that focus to accomplish your desired outcome. Neurons that fire together, wire together. Destroying bad neural connections and strengthening empowering neural connections is a powerful skill that can be applied by anyone but is overlooked by almost everyone. We can decide what thoughts we choose to think and what emotions we give our attention to.

A simple change in your beliefs can have a profound influence on how your brain processes data. As you learn new things and create new thoughts, you can write the blueprint of your neural circuitry through your daily routines and rituals. There are no known limits as to how we can affect the ways our brains are wired up. Therefore, a positive mental attitude is essential to your life quality. Eliminate or minimize negative thoughts as they are not productive in your highest quality of life. Use your imagination to access your highest potentials. Access the power of neuroplasticity to change your brain and change your life throughout your lifetime. An attitude of gratitude for this great gift from the Creator will enhance our ability to become our best selves.

We have five physical senses at the conscious level and a sixth sense at the subconscious level that we can use for optimum performance. This explains our mind, our emotional heart, our body, and our soul. The physical body is temporary, but the mind, heart, and soul are eternal.

Exercise and physical activity improve brain health. Healthy activity improves attention, decision-making, and working memory. The medial temporal lobes contain the hippocampus and are the core of our memory center. Physical activity keeps this part of the brain functional even as we age. This allows newer interconnections in the brain for high performance. Neural flexibility gained by exercising a few times a week leads directly to memory flexibility. Exercise at every age increases brain efficiency.

## Short-Term Memory, Working Memory, and Long-Term Memory

Memory is the component of the brain that stores data and information. Memory is stored in the cerebral cortex, which is the highest part of the brain. The hippocampus is the part of the brain that accesses long-term memory and decides if something should be short term or become long term.

## Short-Term Memory

Short-term memory is useful for only seconds or at most minutes. It usually involves using information to conduct a non-repetitive task to accomplish something of short duration. An example is a text alert for a two-factor authentication that has a one-time only value.

## Working Memory

Working memory is a cognitive system with a limited capacity that can hold information temporarily. Working memory is important for reasoning and the guidance of decision-making and behavior. Working memory is often used synonymously with short-term memory, but the two forms of memory are distinct. Working memory allows for the manipulation of stored information, whereas short-term memory only refers to the short-term storage of information.

Working memory is a theoretical concept central to cognitive psychology, neuropsychology, and neuroscience. Working memory is a form of memory that allows a person to temporarily hold a limited amount of information at the ready for immediate mental use. It is considered essential for learning, problem-solving, and other mental processes. The representation of various kinds of information (such as visual or verbal details) in working memory seems to depend on parts of the cerebral cortex that engage in the perception and long-term memory of those kinds of information. The prefrontal cortex, a part of the brain linked to cognitive control, is thought to play a key role in managing the current contents of working memory, regardless of type. An example of working memory is making a recipe from scratch that you have created over time. The pleasant memory of the taste of the finished product and the good times that you enjoyed with family and friends are examples of long-term memory as a result of the working memory you have.

## Long-Term Memory

The main difference between short-term and long-term memory is that short-term memory stores data temporarily while long-term memory stores data permanently. While short-term memory is volatile, long-term memory is nonvolatile. Since the hippocampus is in the temporal lobe, the temporal lobe helps to form long-term memories and processes new information by the formation of visual and verbal memories. The hippocampus processes new memories into long-term storage. All diverse types of information that you perceive go to different parts of the brain. After the brain perceives all that information, it travels to the hippocampus, which integrates all that information and forms a memory. It also decides whether you need to remember this information now or later.

---

## Chapter 1 Summary:
## Brain Basics: Understanding the Seat of Thought

WE ARE FEARFULLY and wonderfully made by our Creator. Our brain has three main components. Our midbrain is for sensory perception and assists with memory to send impulses to the forebrain for us to reason and think about what to feel and do, while our hindbrain continues to care for the automated functions such as breathing and heartbeat.

When the three main portions of the brain work together, they do so with electrical impulses over complex pathways with chemical releases dependent upon what is happening in the world around us. While this is occurring, naturally produced chemicals are released based on our perception of what is happening around us. There are happy chemicals and unhappy chemicals.

When we are happy with setting a desirable goal, our brain releases the chemical known as dopamine. We love the rush we get when we set and achieve a goal because of this chemical. That is how games on a device keep us engaged. Game creators understand that our brain happiness will keep us going almost to an addictive level of engagement. We love a good dopamine rush. Additionally, serotonin can keep our mood stable with a feeling of happiness and wellbeing. So now dopamine is released when we set and reach a goal combined with serotonin to regulate our mood and assist our overall body health.

Oxytocin, sometimes referred to as the love hormone, is a third happy brain chemical and is released during childbirth and as a response to sexual activity. A nursing mother also experiences an oxytocin release as she holds the child near and naturally feeds the child from her breast. Oxytocin is a social-bonding happy chemical. Oxytocin is believed to have a significant role in social learning and loving each other. Combined with serotonin, we feel safe, happy, and secure.

Then there is the unhappy chemical known as cortisol. Its job is to warn you of danger and stressful situations. This is your fight-or-flight hormone. It is a steroid chemical triggered by stress and survives in your body longer than the happy chemicals. Hormones are chemicals that coordinate different functions in your body by carrying messages through your blood to your organs, skin, muscles, and other tissues. These signals tell your body what to do and when to do it.

Power Thinkers and thought leaders know that regardless of what is happening, they can be in control of their thoughts and moods and that, by selecting what to think about, they can control how they feel. They know that they can rewire their brain for optimum effectiveness. They also know that they can use that power at will. They understand how the brain works and they work it to their advantage. This is what sets them apart from average thinkers.

2
___

# EXECUTIVE STEWARDSHIP: USING MINDSET FOR MASTERING LEADERSHIP

*Brains operate...not by logic but by pattern recognition. This process is not precise, as is logic and mathematics. Instead, it trades off specificity and precision, if necessary, to increase its range. It is likely, for example, that early human thought preceded by metaphor, which, even with the late acquisition of precise means such as logic and mathematical thought, continues to be a major source of imagination and creativity in adult life.*

— GERALD EDELMAN, NOBEL PRIZE

LAUREATE

Prefrontal cortex activity is where we reason with logic. This is the sizable portion of our brain. However, logic may not always be reasonable and must be continually examined for wisdom. Emotions are our spirit. Chapter 8 goes into this in greater detail, but to introduce emotional brain functions, consider the following: The soul is the spiritual nature of humankind and is also the emotional power behind our actions. The mind is our faculty of thinking, reasoning, and applying knowledge. It is human consciousness that starts in the brain and is manifested through our thoughts, actions, emotions, will, memory, and imagination. Our minds are where we decide how to act, what we should do, and how we should do it. Our minds invoke the conscience and our thought processes. In the physical body, the brain coordinates movements, feelings, and distinct functions of the body. The brain is to the body what the conscience is to the soul. The mind works in both. The soul is our eternal spiritual being that currently occupies our temporal and very intricate human body while we are on this earth. Our mind is shared by both the brain and the soul. Memory in the brain and conscience in the soul help us to reflect before acting and then act while guided by our physical memory and our spiritual conscience.

## Mind Has Two Parts: Conscious and Subconscious

Our conscious thoughts are stimulated by the five physical senses and engage when we are awake. Our subconscious thoughts are stimulated in our spirit or sixth sense and are constantly working whether awake or asleep. The executive ability of our brain involves reason and logic and is executed in our conscious state. We can receive thought stimuli based upon outside sources. The outside source for the subconscious mind is from the spiritual realm and thought stimulation. We receive two kinds of stimuli, one is good and the other is evil. Hence the motivation to do good and the enticement to do evil.

How do we know the difference between a good stimulus and an evil stimulus? Consider whether the stimulus is meant to strengthen us or to deceive us, destroy us, and move us away from doing good. Our brain and our conscience process all stimuli and, through the power of thought, either accepts them or rejects them. We can do either, depending upon how we exercise the control of our thoughts. Sometimes we are stronger with our will than at other times, but by forming the right thought habits, we are more likely to make the right choice not just by logic but more importantly by wisdom. Even still, sometimes the stimulus may be recognized for its source, and we allow our physical senses to overcome our mental reasoning and take regrettable action. Experience, wisdom, and willpower are useful in making correct choices. In Chapter 8 we discuss the intricacies of willpower.

How do we know what we should believe? This is where our mind decides actions in the physical world and is influenced by our heart. Our heart is the seat of our emotions and values. Our emotions in conjunction with our reasoning capabilities determine our willpower based upon our desires. This also helps determine our morals and ethics. Keep in mind that the emotions are not always subject to reason, but they are always subject to action.

People rely on their intuition when they suspend analytic thought and go with their inner feelings, sometimes referred to as gut feelings. These feelings are processed by the brain based upon past knowledge or experience. Intuition is a form of knowledge that appears in consciousness without obvious deliberation. It is not magical but rather a faculty in which hunches are generated by the subconscious mind rapidly sifting through experience and cumulative knowledge. Scientists have repeatedly demonstrated how information can register on the brain without conscious awareness and positively influence decision-making and other behavior.

## Verifying Truth and Accurate Thinking

"Accurate thinking" is thinking that is precise and correct. An accurate thinker is cognizant of personal biases, which everyone possesses, and can critically examine facts to achieve conformity to truth consistently. Accuracy is verified when the results over time are both true and consistent. But is our truth what we want something to be, or are we willing to listen to fact with an unbiased mind? Are we seeking to find a way to prove or support what we want an outcome to be, or are we truly looking with an open mind to find and verify something as being true? Will we listen to political rhetoric proliferated by media, or will we do our own research and thinking? Truth is foundational and valuable. Once we know truth, we are free from falsehood. But just how do we discover truth? The following is an interesting story about how one man took the journey to find truth and what he did on the journey.

In 1932, Herbert J. Taylor set out to save the Club Aluminum Products distribution company from bankruptcy. His recovery plan started with changing the ethical climate of the company. He believed the first job was to set policies for the company that would reflect the high ethics and morals God would want in any business. What they needed was a simple, easily remembered guide to right conduct—a sort of ethical yardstick —which everyone in the company could memorize and apply to what they thought, said, and did.

He searched through many books for the answer to their need, but the right phrases eluded him, so he turned to the One who has all the answers. He leaned over his desk, rested his head in his hands, and prayed. After a few moments, he wrote down the twenty-four words that had come to him. Here are the words:

1. Is it the truth?
2. Is it fair to all concerned?
3. Will it build goodwill and better friendships?
4. Will it be beneficial to all concerned?"

Taylor called it "the Four-Way Test of the things we think, say or do."

First testing it out on himself, he realized that the first question, "Is it the truth?" was barely applied in his day-to-day business operations. After sixty days, Herbert J. Taylor decided to share those principles with the four department directors of his company (each had a different religious faith). Those four directors validated his principles and rolled it out company-wide.

When studying his advertising statements, he realized how extraordinarily little could be stated as "truth," so a lot of copywriting adjustments were made to realign the company's messages with a sense of genuine truth. The aggressiveness toward competition was also scrutinized and eliminated.

In 1932, Taylor's company was on the edge of bankruptcy. Twenty years later, by applying the Four-Way Test, the company repaid its debts, generously paid its shareholders, and had a healthy financial balance.

Eleven years later in the 1940s, when Taylor was an

international director of Rotary, he offered the Four-Way Test to the organization, and it was adopted by Rotary for its internal and promotional use. Never changed, the twenty-four-word test remains today a central part of the permanent Rotary structure throughout the world and is held as the standard by which all behavior should be measured. The test has been promoted around the world and is used in myriad forms to encourage personal and business ethical practices. Taylor gave Rotary International the right to use the test in the 1940s and the copyright in 1954. He retained the rights to use the test for himself, his Club Aluminum company, and the Christian Workers Foundation.[1]

These twenty-four words will assist anyone in determining how to know whether something is true or not. For many years, I was a Rotarian, and we recited the Four-Way Test each week at our meetings. I have heard many members in conversation explain what an impact this short but effective exercise has in their individual businesses and daily lives. Truth is powerful once discovered and followed. The pursuit of truth in a business or teamwork is different from truth about something physical. That is why an additional method of truth-seeking is based on research of wisdom and of physical realities. This led to the development of the scientific method.

**Scientific Method**

One definition of the scientific method is a thought and discovery process using principles and procedures for the systematic pursuit of knowledge involving the recognition and formulation of a problem, the collection of data through observation and experiment, and the formulation and testing of hypotheses is known as the scientific method. The scientific method allows scientists to stick to facts and to avoid the influence of preconceived notions and personal biases in research processes, improving the credibility of research findings. The scientific method minimizes the influence of firsthand experiences and cultural beliefs on the experimenter.

Science is the state of knowing: knowledge as distinguished from ignorance or misunderstanding. A scientist is a person who studies something intently. A scientist tries to understand how our world, or other things, work. Scientists make observations, ask questions, and do extensive research in finding the answers to their hypothesis that they are verifying. Scientists are thinkers seeking verifiable truth. All scientists have some type of specialization, such as the human body or the oceans, which provides them with more formal and specific titles. The scientific method guides the pursuit of truth and knowledge. There are as many as seven steps in the scientific method. Another model uses six steps, and another model uses only four steps. In any case, the objective is to determine facts as truth. Here we examine a simple four-step approach.

The first step of the scientific method involves seeing something that interests you. The aim of all scientific methods is the same—that is, to analyze the observation made at the beginning —and there are various steps adopted as per the requirement of any given observation. However, there is a generally accepted sequence of steps of scientific methods. A simple approach is to observe what you are interested in, ask questions about what you have observed, form a hypothesis based upon your observations, conduct experiments to evaluate your hypothesis, consider the results, and draw a conclusion.

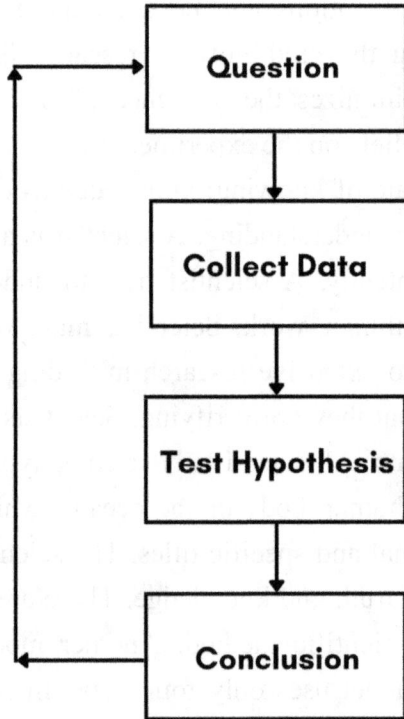

```
        ┌──────────────────┐
   ┌───▶│    Question      │
   │    └──────────────────┘
   │            │
   │            ▼
   │    ┌──────────────────┐
   │    │   Collect Data   │
   │    └──────────────────┘
   │            │
   │            ▼
   │    ┌──────────────────┐
   │    │  Test Hypothesis │
   │    └──────────────────┘
   │            │
   │            ▼
   │    ┌──────────────────┐
   └────│   Conclusion     │
        └──────────────────┘
```

**1. Observation and formulation of a question:** This is the first step of the scientific method. To start, an observation must be made into any observable aspect or phenomena of the universe and a question needs to be asked pertaining to that aspect. It is important to ask the right question. Additional experiments must be performed as additional questions appear.

**2. Data collection and hypothesis:** The next step involved in the scientific method is to collect all related data and formulate a hypothesis based on the observation. A hypothesis is an assumption that is made based on some evidence as revealed in the question. The hypothesis could be the cause of the phenomena, its effect, or its relation to any other phenomena. It must be clear and concise.

**3. Testing the hypothesis:** After the hypothesis is formed, it needs to be tested scientifically by conducting experiments. The aim of these experiments is to figure out whether the hypothesis agrees with or contradicts the observations made in the real world. The confidence in the hypothesis increases or decreases based on the result of the experiments. Power Thinkers conduct thought experiments in much the same way.

**4. Analysis and Conclusion:** This step involves the use of proper mathematical and other scientific procedures to verify the results of the experiment. Based on the analysis, the future course of action can be determined. If the data found in the analysis is consistent with the hypothesis, it is accepted. If not, then it is rejected or changed and analyzed again and again as necessary.

It must be remembered that a hypothesis cannot be proved or disproved by doing one experiment. It needs to be experimented repeatedly until there are no discrepancies in the data and the result. When there are no discrepancies and the hypothesis is proved beyond any doubt, it is accepted as a theory. A theory is assumed to be true until proven otherwise. When the theory is tested by a wide variety of experimenters and they reach a consensus about it, it is generally accepted as truth.

The scientific method can also be accomplished by defining a problem, stating an objective to discover, formulating tentative solutions, collecting data and information, classifying, analyzing, interpreting these items, and drawing conclusions. The scientific method employs a mindset that constantly is challenging, weighing, and explaining—one that continually asks "why?" The scientific method implies objectivity rather than subjectivity; it implies selectivity and discrimination, and it implies creativity.

Power Thinkers likely follow a proven process such as the scientific method to methodically arrive at their conclusions. It takes a disciplined approach to reach conclusions that are truth. Proven facts are evidence of truth. Truth is defined as that which conforms with fact or reality. It is genuineness, veracity, or actuality. In a word, truth is reality. It is how things actually are, not just as they appear.

## Thinking

Cognition is thinking, which is a mental action or process of acquiring knowledge and understanding through thought, experience, and the senses. Metacognition is thinking about one's thinking. It is a form of higher order thinking consisting of skills that are important to learning. Your executive brain functions allow you to pause, be aware, and be mindful about the things you are thinking about. Consider this question, "what could you be thinking about, if you were not thinking about....?" This question often helps redirect our mind to something that is more important for us to dwell upon and consider.

Higher order thinking skills include synthesis of thought by combining ideas to form a theory or to develop a system. Higher order thinking also involves analyzing the structure of the thing under consideration and then using the mind to reason with logic the possibilities of the application or existence of the thing under consideration. Once an understanding is discovered, an experiment is conducted to evaluate and or apply the outcome of the thought. In this way, higher order thinking skills are very similar to the scientific method.

Cognition includes knowledge about when and how to use strategies for learning or problem-solving. Metacognition also involves thinking about one's own thinking process such as study skills, memory capabilities, and the ability to monitor learning. Metacognitive knowledge is about one's own cognitive processes and the understanding of how to regulate those processes to maximize learning.

Metacognitive knowledge can include a variety of types of knowledge. Consider content knowledge (declarative knowledge), which is understanding one's own capabilities. A thinker can evaluate their own knowledge of something they learned. Because this involves an individual evaluation it is possible that not all metacognition is correct. Care should be given that content rather than performance is the main consideration. The aim is accuracy, not level of performance.

Task knowledge is procedural knowledge or know-how. This is a person's ability to evaluate the difficulty of a task related to their overall performance on the task as previously performed or learned.

Strategic knowledge (conditional knowledge) is one's own capability for using strategies to learn information. An accurate thinker strives to choose a strategy that will verify knowledge.

Thinking is not easy. It requires physical and mental energy. Periodic rest is important in the thinking process just like exercise of our physical and mental capabilities is important to provide the necessary energy for thinking. By taking time to retreat, reflect, and renew, we can develop the strength and stamina to be Power Thinkers. The one who succeeds is the one who is willing to do the things that unsuccessful people are unwilling to do. Are you willing to put forth the effort required to think and succeed?

## Thoughts

All thoughts trigger a brain chemical release, which depending upon those thoughts, is a positive or negative stimulus. Thoughts are energy in electric form.

There is a trigger (stimulus), a thought, an action, and a consequence. We have some ability to reason this pathway but not always the strength to choose the action that gives the most positive consequence. Strength is gained by repetition and a habit of thought. Consistent action compounds over time. It all begins with our thoughts, which are the antecedent of action.

As we learned in Chapter 1, every thought releases a brain chemical response. The pleasure chemical, dopamine, can be released by our satisfaction of having done good or bad. We must train our values and reinforce them. Power Thinking requires not only intellectual study but also the innate talent with which each person is gifted. The techniques are the same regardless of intelligence.

One must keep their mind on the things they want and off the things they don't want. Control your attention and give good thought to what you really want.

**Ensuring Wisdom Over Logic**

Our mind is the processor of thought and decision maker of action. Decisions are made in the mind with knowledge, understanding, and wisdom. Wisdom supersedes all foolishness, and wisdom is supreme. But how do we know what is wise?

Russel Ackoff, professor emeritus of management science at the Wharton School, University of Pennsylvania, gave us insight on the journey from data to wisdom. This helps us recognize the journey of thought to discover wisdom. Wisdom is at the top of the hierarchy. Descending from wisdom, there is understanding, knowledge, information, and, at the bottom, data. Each of these includes the categories that fall below it—for example, there can be no wisdom without understanding and no understanding without knowledge. Data are products of observation and are of less value until they are pieced together to make sense as information.

Information is the who, what, when, where, and how and is comprised of data. While information is inferred from data, data do not become information until they are combined in meaningful ways much like a metallic ore is refined to a usable form. However, not all information or data constructs are relevant. One must learn to sift out the irrelevant information and not be overwhelmed by it. To do that, one must observe a problem at the basic level with the fewest number of variables to explain it and then, with this identified clarity, make sense of the data as information that is relevant to the problem. Quantum physics and quantum mechanics adhere to this principle. In this case, less is more. This begs the question as to why anyone would want to make a data-driven decision when a better decision is a data-informed decision.

Knowledge is "know-how," for example, how a system works. It is what makes possible the transformation of information into instructions. It makes control of a system possible to solve a problem. To control a system is to make it work efficiently. Efficiency is doing things right. To increase efficiency is either to increase the probability of producing a desired outcome with fixed resources or to decrease the number of resources required to produce it with a specified probability.

Knowledge can be obtained in these ways: by transmission from another who has it, by instruction, or by extracting it from experience. In any case, the acquisition of knowledge is teaming information with knowledge to develop an understanding. The ability to acquire knowledge on one's own is intelligence that is genuine and not artificial which is produced by machines. It comes about from learning and adaptation. Learning takes place when one's efficiency increases over time or trials. It can take place when the conditions that affect relevant efficiency either remain constant or hit a target increase. When the relevant conditions change, new learning is required to maintain or increase efficiency. Such learning is called adaptation.

Artificial intelligence (AI) should augment human intelligence but not replace it. While it was strictly human intelligence that created the machines that can compute faster and with accuracy, machines are meant only to augment and enhance human effort, not run free without human judgment and the exercise of wisdom. The question of whether AI will replace human workers assumes that AI and humans have the same qualities and abilities —but they do not. AI-based machines are fast, more accurate, and consistently rational, but they are not intuitive, emotional, or culturally sensitive. And it is exactly these abilities that humans possess and which make us effective. Remember, effectiveness is doing the right thing. Human abilities are more expansive. Contrary to AI abilities that are only responsive to the data available, humans can imagine, anticipate, feel, and judge changing situations, which allows them to shift from short-term to long-term concerns. These abilities are unique to humans and do not require a steady flow of externally provided data to work as is the case with artificial intelligence.

Humans have authentic intelligence rather than artificial intelligence. In a *Harvard Business Review* March 2021 article, David De Cremer (professor, National University of Singapore) and Garry Kasparov (chess grandmaster and former World Chess Champion) ran an experiment allowing humans to use computers in a chess match. Previously, Kasparov was beaten by an IBM computer using Deep Blue software. Their premise was that the computer could augment human judgment and strategy thinking without replacing it. They developed the term "augmented intelligence" as a third "AI" way of thinking that engages the efficiency and speed of a machine to team with the wisdom of judgment of a human that is collaborative in nature, but it is also clear that it represents a collaborative effort in service of humans. Remember data, information, and knowledge increase understanding and efficiency, but it is wisdom that increases effectiveness. Effectiveness is doing the right thing, not to be confused with efficiency, which is doing the thing right. Excellence occurs only when both effectiveness and efficiency are in concert with one another. The formula for excellence is the combination of both efficiency and effectiveness. In other words, efficiency (doing things right) combined with effectiveness (doing the right thing) are both needed to produce excellence. Therefore, augmented intelligence can lead to excellence collaboratively and quickly with the efficiency of machines in collaboration with the effectiveness of human thought. Another way to say it is that authentic intelligence combined with artificial intelligence can produce augmented intelligence through the power of thought, that is, Power Thinking.

Learning and adaptation may take place by trial and error or systematically by detection of error and its correction. Diagnosis is the identification of the cause of error, and prescription is instruction directed at its correction. Systematic learning and adaptation require understanding error, knowing why it was made, and how to correct it. Learning, adaptation, knowledge, and understanding focus on efficiency, not effectiveness. Effectiveness is more important than efficiency. You can be doing the wrong thing in a very efficient way, but it is not the right thing to do. That is why if you must choose one over the other, always choose effectiveness. Then excellence can occur over time by doing the right thing in the right way.

Intelligence is the ability to increase efficiency; wisdom is the ability to increase effectiveness. Power Thinking enables one to develop intelligence with applied wisdom to produce excellence.

Understanding requires diagnosis and prescription. This requires the application of knowledge, which is know-how over time until the results of application are predictable. Information, like news, ages relatively rapidly. Knowledge has a longer life span, although inevitably it too becomes obsolete. Understanding has an aura of permanence about it. Wisdom, unless lost, is permanent; it becomes a permanent endowment unless it is not followed.

As previously noted, information, knowledge, and understanding all focus on efficiency. Wisdom adds value, which requires the mental function known as judgment. Evaluations of efficiency all are based on a logic which, in principle, can be specified and therefore can be programmed and automated. These principles are general and impersonal. We can speak of the efficiency of an act independent of the actor. Not so for judgment. Judgment is an individual and personal thing that can be acquired over time by everyone. Efficiency is inferable from proper grounds; ethical and aesthetic values are not. They are unique and personal.

Information, like news, ages relatively rapidly. Knowledge has a longer life span, although inevitably it too becomes obsolete. Understanding has an aura of permanence about it. Wisdom, unless lost, is permanent; it becomes a permanent endowment. Hence the term "wisdom of the ages." Knowledge and understanding are valuable, but wisdom is the most valuable of all. Wisdom has sometimes been described as knowing when something should be done and when is the right time to apply knowledge with understanding. Wisdom enables one to design the future and not just apply what has happened in the past. Wisdom also enables one to design what should be done. Wisdom gives one the ability to see and evaluate the long-term consequences of one's actions.

The mind is the gatekeeper to the heart. It receives a message and exercises judgment, which makes it the seat of thought. It also informs our conscience and develops values and commitment over time. We know that thought always precedes action. That is why so many people want to get into one's thoughts so that they can stimulate or control a person's actions. The wise thinker uses the mind and heart combined with volitional will to act according to conscience.

Heart is comprised of the power of will where determination

and resolve are formed based upon understanding by the mind that enables one to act with wisdom.

When examining the continuum of data to wisdom and when considering the executive function of the brain, it is also useful to examine efficiency, effectiveness, and excellence in application of wisdom. For example, data, information, knowledge, and understanding contribute to doing things right, which is efficiency. They also give awareness as to what can be done. Wisdom is the level of thought that contributes to doing the right thing, which is effectiveness. With wisdom you can know what is best and know when and why then to apply knowledge with understanding. It is with wisdom that you can develop a vision and a design for what gives new meaning and gives insight into new meaning. It is with wisdom that the brain can be unlocked to discover the unknown because at this level you can design what should be done, which produces excellence.

## Mindsets

A person can set their mind to fixate on an idea, value, or way of thinking. They also could set their mind to be a constant learner thereby growing in their knowledge, understanding, and wisdom. Mindsets are based upon thought habits and experiences, which produce behaviors and actions with a result.

An open or growth mindset understands that important qualities can be cultivated and changed substantially. An open mindset thinks about new ways to confront obstacles and thinks about how to stretch themselves. A closed mindset person believes you are who you are and nothing can be done about it even if you do things differently. They are always trying to prove themselves and are super sensitive about being wrong or making mistakes.

Consider the differences in an average mindset and an elite mindset.

| Average Mindset | Elite Mindset |
|---|---|
| - Makes an excuse<br>- Sees confidence as a feeling<br>- Uses the phrase "have to"<br>- Says it is impossible<br>- Feels sorry for themselves<br>- Sees failure as final<br>- Focuses on what they can't control<br>- Wears their emotions on their sleeve | - Makes it happen<br>- Knows confidence<br>- Uses the words "get to" or "want to"<br>- Focuses on how they act and need to do<br>- Says it is going to be very difficult<br>- Are focused on others, not themselves<br>- Focuses on what they can control<br>- Never shows weakness<br>- Displays confident body language |

Consider this question: When do you feel smart, when you are flawless or when you are learning? Growth thinkers thrive when stretching themselves. Fixed thinkers feel smart when things are safely within their grasp. This determines their interest level. Interest levels drive thought. Power Thinking is for growth mindsets. Success is about learning, not about proving you are smart. Growth mindsets continue to learn while fixed mindsets are content with what they already know and resist learning new things. George Leonard in his book *Mastery* became a black belt in martial arts, but when he changed fields, he became a white belt again so he could learn and master something new.

Fixed mindsets find comfort with the answers when they do not make any mistakes, when they finish something fast and it is perfect, and when something is easy for them but other people cannot do it. It's about being perfect right now.

Growth mindset thinkers look for opportunities: when it is hard, they try really hard and then can do something they couldn't do before; when they work on something for a long time and then start to figure it out. For them it's not about immediate perfection; it's about learning something over time, confronting a challenge, and making progress.

## Setting Your Mind Is Your Choice

If you are not intentionally training your mind, your mindset becomes a result of what others feed you. Feed your own mind with wise inputs not mental junk food. Be aware of where your mind is focused and then be willing to work on it. You must control your mindset before you can control your performance.

## How to Set Your Mind

First, have an open mind—realize that you can conceive, believe, and achieve whatever you genuinely set your mind to do. Set your heart and then set your mind. It starts with the heart (desire). This gives you a motive for action based upon strong emotion. Imagine what you want to do or desire to do. Set your mind by focusing on something until it becomes what you do. Be alert and clear-minded as you set your mind on something. Don't let anyone or anything discourage you or distract you.

## Executive Stewardship

Executive stewardship suggests a dichotomy of an administrative function. Executives contribute to the performance of the organization, while stewards manage another's property or other affairs. Organizationally, some people are in leadership positions, and some are in management positions. In fact, a whole-brain thinker can lead or manage as the situation dictates. An executive steward is one who leads people and manages things. The application to Power Thinking is that when you are leading people, use the creative right hemisphere of the brain which also involves sensitivity and feelings of kindness and strength. At the same time be aware of the need to use the logical left hemisphere of the brain when organizing thoughts for action combined with controlled attention for accomplishment.

This same dichotomy also exists in the respective functions of the left and right hemispheres of the brain. The left side is responsible for the concrete sequential and logical functions of the brain whereas the right side is responsible for the sensitive, intuitive, and creative functions.

People sometimes are characterized by their dominant cognitive functions as "left-brained" or "right-brained." Where such polarity exists, one sees either a narrow-minded thinker or a scatter-brained thinker. A Power Thinker administers their power of thought with discernment, insight, discretion, understanding, wisdom, perseverance, and self-control. A Power Thinker knows when to use imagination and creativity and when to administer critical and analytical thinking with an understanding of the functions of the left brain and of the right brain through the administration of the faculty of thought.

## Master Mind Alliance

The concept of the "master mind alliance" was introduced by Napoleon Hill in his book from the 1920s, *The Law of Success*, and expanded upon in his 1930s book, *Think and Grow Rich*. While Napoleon Hill called it a "master mind alliance," it's been shortened and modernized to "mastermind group." Mastermind groups offer a combination of brainstorming, education, peer accountability, and support in a group setting to sharpen your business and personal skills. A mastermind group helps you and your mastermind group members achieve success. Members challenge each other to set strong goals and more importantly, to accomplish them. Hill suggested that this could be done both in person and by reading and knowing the innermost thoughts of historical figures as well. It really is a matter of sharing thoughts and philosophies. The power of it is that as a result of considering other people's thoughts, a new thought is created that is better and newer than either of the individuals had previously thought. The main purpose of the mastermind alliance is to create a synergy of thought, which is more powerful than an individual thought. This is particularly true when those thoughts are focused on a particular decisive definite goal with intentional purpose. Some members of a mastermind group may be emotionally closer than others for any number of reasons. In those cases, a mind meld may occur.

Mind meld is when two minds combine their expertise to achieve maximum results. Some people call this mental telepathy due to the process of transferring thought from one mind to another without the need to use speech, writing, or other normal signals. It is a direct communication of thoughts and feelings between people's minds. Often people have made statements like "you must have read my mind" or "how did you know I was thinking of that?" Humans cannot literally read the minds of others but can create mental models to effectively intuit people's thoughts and feelings. This is known as empathic accuracy, and it involves "reading" cues telegraphed by the words, emotions, and body language of another person. This occurs when certain members of the mastermind group are more intent on the focused thought than any others. This then is when two or more people are obsessed with the discovery and implementation of a particular purpose.

Great thinking comes when good thoughts are shaped in a collaborative environment. In order to achieve maximum leadership, one needs to learn to recognize and promote the best ideas no matter where or from whom they come. One way is to listen to all ideas. This is especially important during a brainstorming session. Shutting down any ideas might prevent you from discovering a great idea. During these sessions, some ideas will sound crazy on the surface but may, upon further consideration, produce a very important concept. There is synergy in a group think or think tank, as some call it. Synergy occurs when the combined effect is greater than the sum of the parts. It is possible that when one hears another person's idea, it is interpreted in a new and different way than when the originator thought about it or expressed it. That then produces a third idea that neither person would have had if it had not been expressed and therefore provoked new thinking. The more ideas, the better the outcome.

Cultivation of attentiveness as a daily discipline can lead to new ideas or practices that can improve what you are trying to do. This is a state of mind that is always perceiving things for creative thoughtful interpretation and innovation. Ideas are intangible forces, but they have more power than the physical brains that give birth to them. They have the power to live on after the brain that created them has returned to dust. The US Constitution is an example of such power and of a mastermind alliance.

## Using All Skills

Effective administration of thought is a whole-brain activity. The left side of the brain is dominant in the management function because management is a function imposed on things, such as the procedural knowledge of any task. On the other hand, the right side of the brain dominates when the leadership function engages because leadership involves people, not things. This is an important understanding when engaging in a Master Mind Alliance. Without sensitivity, one cannot be an effective consensus builder.

Team Building activities, motivational and inspirational activities, and judgments of fairness and equity are important leadership skills. Neuro-leadership involves a keen sense of the emotional levels and status of members of the team so as to keep the brain open. Remember, stress causes the amygdala to tighten and the hippocampus to restrict, which affects short-term memory, working memory, and long-term memory. This also restricts the creative and imaginative mood of the teammates.

There will always be tense times due to human nature, but being aware of neuroscience allows a leader to not only understand what is happening in their own brain but be attuned to what is happening in the minds of the team members. This then helps to navigate change that can occur, perhaps should occur, but will be difficult to manage without the insight that neuroscience provides the leader. Keep in mind that change is always occurring. As a result, better decisions can be made, more difficult problems can be solved, and the sense of belonging to an excellent high performing team will build loyalty. That is when the happy brain chemicals that were discussed in Chapter 1 are released in the brains of team members. A Power Thinker and thought leader will be mindful of these critical elements of success.

Executive stewardship manifests whole-brain activity. The left hemisphere commences when the management of things is necessary, and the right hemisphere commences when leadership is called for. This is the practice of executive stewardship. The executive steward engages both hemispheres in collaboration to articulate and accomplish the organizational mission.

An executive steward engages both the left and right hemispheres of the brain to articulate and accomplish whatever they or their organization sets their minds to do. This occurs in the executive portion of the brain known as the cerebrum as discussed in Chapter 1. The executive steward engages both hemispheres in collaboration to articulate and accomplish a purpose whether it is personal or organizational.

By adopting a definite major purpose, you have selected an object on which you have to focus your controlled attention. While it is possible to have more than one goal, there is danger in the loss of focus when more than two or three goals are attempted. Fewer goals can be achieved with excellence. One may still reach multiple goals, but the number of those achieved with excellence diminishes as the number of goals worked on at the same time increases. The reason for this is focus and controlled attention due to an understanding of priorities. Secondary priorities should not take away from the most important priorities. Controlled attention is the act of coordinating all the faculties of the mind and directing their combined power to a given end. You can do anything, but you can't do everything at the same time.

## Controlled Attention at Work

Chemistry teaches us that each individual element can combine to form new substances that are quite different from the components that constitute them. Water is a simple example: Both oxygen and hydrogen are gasses, but when two hydrogen atoms combine with one oxygen atom, they form a liquid, and an incredibly useful one at that. Sodium and chlorine are volatile and dangerous in their pure states, but when one atom of each form a pair, they become ordinary table salt.

The same is true of thought. Thoughts of one nature can combine with those of another sort, and controlled attention is how you decide the process. If you see a threatening situation, fear for safety and desire for wellbeing will combine into thoughts of action, leading you to escape the harmful situation. Both the initial thoughts are strong, but it is the combination of the two that is strongest and most effective at preventing harm.

When you approach accomplishment with a combination of strategies in your mind, you can produce powerful results. Begin by being crystal clear in your mind of exactly what you are to accomplish. This makes it easy to decide what action should be taken. Next, exercise the discipline required to move forward even when you don't necessarily feel like it. Do this by reviewing your purpose and affirming your commitment to it and the details that you have developed.

Once the purpose is set, a regular affirmation of the purpose by reviewing it multiple times per day will create a neural pathway which strengthens this habit of thought and also creates a strong desire to focus on the accomplishment of the purpose. The stronger the neural pathway, the more automatic the action due to force of habit.

This helps develop a willpower that is actively engaged and directed toward your purpose. Remember, will is the soul exercising its power of self-direction. Will governs and directs the mind. Mind thinks according to the will. Mind governs and directs the body. Volition is the willing power in action. Action leads to accomplishment. Ideas without action lead nowhere.

Focus your mind each day to devote the time and energy required for accomplishment. Focus is the first step of willpower. The will has power to concentrate energy upon a given point. The greater the will, the greater the capacity is developed to provide a clear vision for accomplishment. The starting point of all achievement is desire. Keep this constantly in mind. Give it your undivided attention. Strengthen this daily. The stronger your desire for accomplishment, the stronger will be the result. Power Thinking develops this strength.

It is up to you to decide to act. If not you, then who? If not now, then when and how? No one can do for you what you can and should do for yourself. New behaviors and new neural pathways can be developed by any individual who takes action to accomplish what is a burning desire or motive for the things they want to accomplish. Consistency compounds. That is true for consistent action or consistent inaction. This is the reason why individual personal initiative is required by a person who has developed the determination to succeed. It depends upon their action to accomplish what they envision as something important to do.

As you create the vision for your journey, ask yourself a "what if" question to begin the journey of creative vision for your goals. Questions beget thinking, which begets creativity, which begets new ideas, which lead to innovation and improvement. Nothing stays the same, and the act of being creative is important for anyone seeking to accomplish great things. It all begins with thinking and becomes exponential with Power Thinking.

Once you believe that you have a clear picture of what you want to accomplish and you have followed the previously mentioned actions, put your belief into action. Faith without work is dead. Ideas that one creates and believes can be accomplished will never come into existence unless they take action for the accomplishment of the idea. The work we do shows the faith that we have in the need and the ability to accomplish what we envision. Faith that is not applied is useless.

Now, pick a problem you need or wish to solve. You can either do nothing or you can apply the previously mentioned strategies to solve it. Purpose (long-term intent based upon values) should not be confused with specific goals or business strategies (which should change frequently as goals are reached). Whereas you might achieve a goal or complete a strategy, you cannot fulfill a purpose; it is like a guiding star on the horizon—forever pursued but never reached. Although purpose itself does not change, it does inspire change. Purpose stimulates change and progress. Personal or organizational direction should create a single unifying principle that connects with one's emotional aspirations. A common purpose is what drives the extra effort, creativity, teamwork, and extraordinary focus.

Your mind is cleared of all fear and doubt. That is self-discipline working through willpower, expressed in applied faith, and acted upon through self-suggestion. This combination of forces will stimulate the imagination and cause it to create the means through which the problem can be solved. Once this happens, of course, it is still up to you to act on that plan to the best of your ability.

Develop the obsession and tenacity of one of the greatest inventors of all time, Thomas Edison. History reveals that Thomas Edison tried ten thousand things that did not work before he invented the incandescent light bulb.[2] Clearly, he was a disciplined Power Thinker.

---

## Chapter 2 Summary:
## Executive Stewardship: Using Mindset for Mastering Leadership

EXECUTIVE FUNCTION IS DECISION-MAKING, and emotion drives action. Brain and mind are part of body and soul. Brain is part of the body, and body is temporarily housing the soul. Mind is a faculty functioning in both the brain and the spirit.

Most of us want truth and accuracy and always strive to find it and live by it. It may be hard to find, but the pursuit of verifiable truth is necessary for a Power Thinker. But then, what is next after we find the truth? How did we determine it? Was it beyond a reasonable doubt? Has it been already established as truth, and do we accept it? Once we determine that something is truth and we decide to live truthfully, we must act wisely.

We discussed how to use data for information, which can lead to knowledge based upon understanding, and then and only then can we act with wisdom. That is why no one should make a data-driven decision. Data can only inform. After that the thinking process is engaged so we can decide what if any action should be taken and how much willpower and energy should be expended. We use our minds in the executive portion of the brain to decide what action to take. Then we exercise the emotion of our willpower to voluntarily do the things in the sequence that should be done to accomplish what we have decided to do. This is our energy source because emotions are always subject to action. Ideally our emotions lead us to action based upon reasoning that occurred in the executive portion of the brain. We then act based upon a mindset that we have developed and when we have set our mind and our heart on the accomplishment.

3

# HOW TO USE YOUR BRAIN FOR POWERFUL CHANGE

*Your brain is like a muscle, use it and make it strong.*

— JESSE NIEBAUM AND SILVIA BUNGE,
PROFESSORS OF PSYCHOLOGY

Have you ever felt like there were two of you? Have you felt like you are moving back and forth in your thoughts from ordinary life and peak possibility? No doubt you have. The negative part of your thoughts thrives on self-limitations, fear, doubt, indecisiveness, and inaction. The positive thoughts feed on faith, courage, confidence in your ability, initiative, enthusiasm, and a strong will to succeed. Which one wins? The one you feed the most.

Psychologists have long believed that within each person are two selves—the one that people can see and that you portray and the one you know deep inside known as your other self or your inner self. Your inner self develops a strong vision of what needs to be done.

## VUCA

This visionary self allows you to thrive in a volatile, uncertain, complex, and ambiguous (VUCA) world. The VUCA world requires visionary leadership to improvise, overcome, and adapt to changing circumstances. Warren Bennis and Burt Nanus first used the term in 1985 in their book *Leaders: The Strategies For Taking Charge*, and the US military began using it in the early 1990s after the end of the Cold War.[1]

Leading people and managing things requires executive stewardship and deep, purposeful, creative thought. Power Thinkers can use such a paradigm as they operate under constantly changing conditions. Because this is a VUCA world, Power Thinkers understand that best practices are in the past while best thinking is needed today and tomorrow. The COVID-19 pandemic has been a worldwide disruptor, not just an interrupter. Interruption merely pauses common activities for a short period of time, then allows them to continue in much the same direction that they were happening. Disruption acts more like a pivot point to change directions. Work choices and conditions changed quickly during the pandemic and are not quickly resuming the same as before. Companies have realized that workers can work remotely from almost anywhere. While it is always good to have face to face interaction, modern technology has facilitated a combination of both face to face and remote work. Therefore, conditions of work and schooling have changed. Changing conditions always need individuals with the commitment to deep thought and creative solutions arrived at timely by a disciplined approach. Power Thinkers will lead the way in recognizing change and in reacting to it with creative solutions.

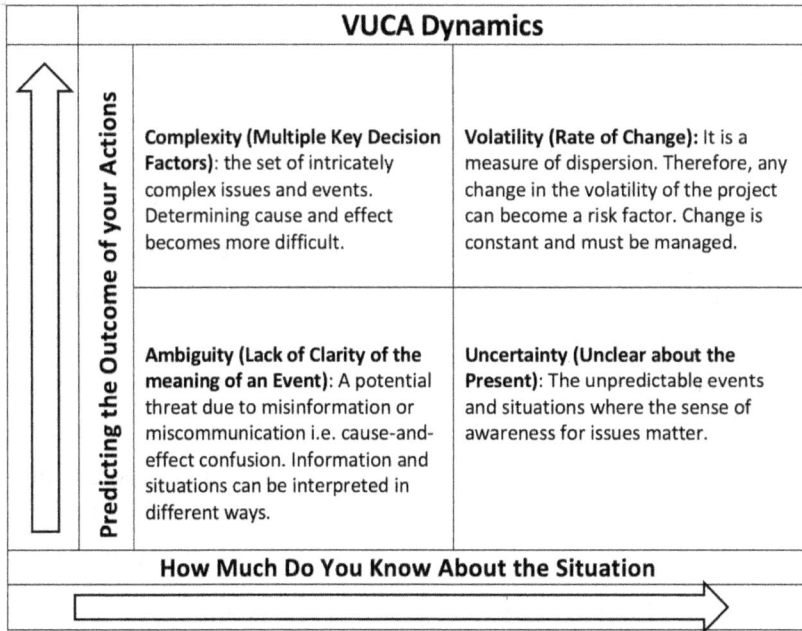

| VUCA Dynamics | | |
|---|---|---|
| **Predicting the Outcome of your Actions** | **Complexity (Multiple Key Decision Factors)**: the set of intricately complex issues and events. Determining cause and effect becomes more difficult. | **Volatility (Rate of Change)**: It is a measure of dispersion. Therefore, any change in the volatility of the project can become a risk factor. Change is constant and must be managed. |
| | **Ambiguity (Lack of Clarity of the meaning of an Event)**: A potential threat due to misinformation or miscommunication i.e. cause-and-effect confusion. Information and situations can be interpreted in different ways. | **Uncertainty (Unclear about the Present)**: The unpredictable events and situations where the sense of awareness for issues matter. |
| | How Much Do You Know About the Situation | |

To thrive in a VUCA world, leaders need to be ready to disrupt and be disrupted. This requires flexibility and the ability to adapt to new circumstances. It also requires that they are careful to interpret current evidence carefully to determine cause and effect as unpredictable events and situations occur and examine how quickly they can occur or are occurring. Power Thinkers are mindful of a VUCA world.

## OODA Loop

Another useful thinking approach during uncertain changing times is the OODA Loop. On May 22, 2018 the Air University

Press first released the book *A Discourse on Winning and Losing,* featuring the OODA concept developed by John Boyd. The book was edited and compiled by Grant T. Hammond. The OODA Loop is the cycle observe–orient–decide–act, developed by military strategist and US Air Force Colonel John Boyd.[2] Boyd challenged air tactic orthodoxy including fighter tactics and how war should be fought. Boyd applied the concept to the combat operations process, often at the operational level during military campaigns. It is now also often applied to understand commercial operations and learning processes. The approach explains how agility can overcome raw power. Colonel John Boyd coined the term OODA Loop, in the 1950s. Colonel Boyd, known as the fighter pilot who changed the art of war, was an F-86 pilot and commander of a fighter group during the latter part of the Korean War. He believed that when at a disadvantage, a competent pilot could still overcome that disadvantage by attacking the mind of his opponent. His observations led him to a greater understanding of human reaction time and the coining of the term OODA Loop. Colonel Boyd trained his pilots based upon his observations of human reaction time, and as a result, his pilots had a 10 to 1 kill ratio over the superior Mig-15s. Whether a quick reaction time is needed in emergency situations or a short pressing deadline is the current challenge, this concept is a useful guide.

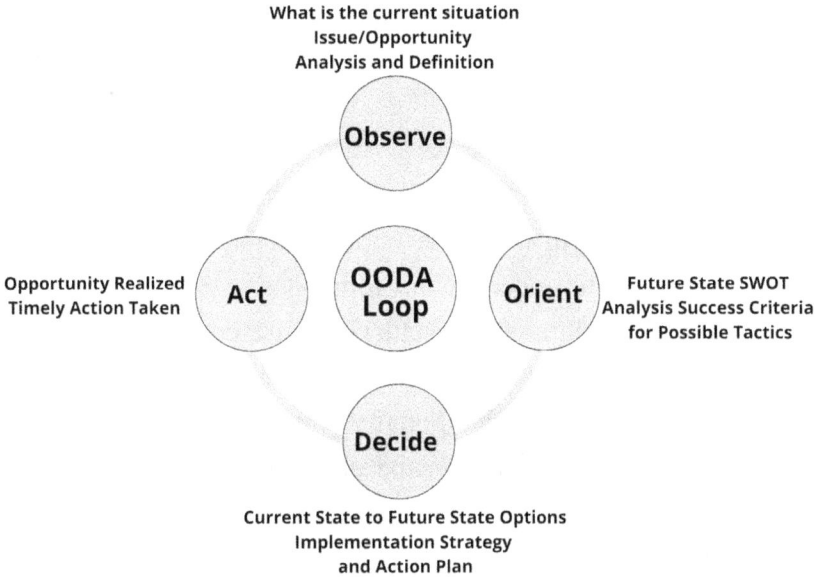

What is the current situation
Issue/Opportunity
Analysis and Definition

**Observe**

Opportunity Realized
Timely Action Taken

**Act**

**OODA Loop**

**Orient**

Future State SWOT
Analysis Success Criteria
for Possible Tactics

**Decide**

Current State to Future State Options
Implementation Strategy
and Action Plan

## Quantum You

The transformative you is the quantum you. Just like the spinning coin, you are the current you and the transformative you at the same time. I was not conformed but transformed by the renewing of my mind. Perhaps you have experienced having a creative thought while resting or even sleeping. I have had this happen to me, and I was compelled to get up and capture the thought before it left me. This is an example of creative vision, which is the inner self. You are who you are as you become the "you" that your creative vision allows you to become. You are constantly spinning in this present life as you move through time. We each have an inner self and it changes over time. The inner self that we currently are while becoming the next inner self as we move through time is our quantum inner self. Our next inner self is being developed as our thoughts make us into our next self. Because of this constant spinning and change, this is our quantum self that is two things at the same time. Change is constant and comes from within and is driven by our innermost thoughts. Instead of human beings, we are human "becomings." We are being transformed as we go through life.

For example, we no doubt have all had the experience of a thought that came to us in the middle of the night. This is an example of how the subconscious mind is always at work. When you give it an assignment, whether you are conscious or semi-conscious, the creative subconscious mind connects with Infinite Intelligence to let specific thoughts emerge. The wise person captures them before they escape and acts on them while the opportunity is available. Not everyone recognizes or captures opportunities. A student of mine once gave me a sign that still hangs in my office. It reads, "Opportunity is often missed because it is disguised as hard work." It reminds me of the need to recognize opportunity, relate it to my current circumstance, assimilate the possibility that is presented and apply my action skillfully to take advantage of the opportunity as a Power Thinker.

## Types of Thought

There are three types of thought:

**1. Conscious thought**: focused thought stimulated by our five physical senses. Things like minding your business, paying attention, being alert.

**2. Unconscious thought**: unfocused thought like daydreaming or mind wandering mindlessly. Things like not minding your business or not paying attention. Just the mind drifting.

**3. Subconscious thought:** thoughts always working under the surface, whether we are consciously or unconsciously thinking about something and we can receive thought stimuli based upon outside sources. The outside source for the subconscious mind is from the spiritual realm. As stated earlier, some of the stimuli is good and some of it is evil. Hence the motivation to do good and/or the enticement to do evil. We must constantly be aware of this.

Your inner self is constantly moving into and out of a conscious or subconscious state. The conscious state is where the five physical senses are most in view. The subconscious state is where we can go beyond the immediate five senses to think while paying more attention to the mind and heart than to the physical body. The conscious mind is dominant when we are awake and fully engaged in the physical world, the subconscious mind is always at work both when we are operating in the phys-ical world stimulus and when we are at rest or asleep. We can access the subconscious mind at will by slowing down the response to physical stimulus and allowing an almost trance-like state to focus on thought uninterrupted by physical stimulus. We can do this while asleep or, with practice, while awake. Accessing the subconscious mind happens sometimes when we disengage from the world around us and go into deep thought with no boundaries. We let our imagination run free and explore a myriad of ideas without judging the outcome of those ideas. This is reverie or free thought. We can direct the subconscious mind to search and find clarity for the best outcome. The subcon-scious mind is where we get a trigger thought from infinite intel-ligence. It is in essence our spiritual world. We each are comprised of our heart, our mind, our body, and our soul or spirit. While in this physical world, we are triggered by the five physical senses while our spiritual self or other self as some have called it, is triggered by ideas, values, beliefs, faith, fact, and feelings or emotions.

Power Thinkers develop disciplined thought habits. Use your imagination and creativity because they are the source of ideas, and ideas matter. Train your focus. It is not enough to know it; you must exercise it. Eliminate the escape hatches. Be all in. Persistence is key because the brain loves to win. Give it a cocktail of happy brain chemicals. The cost is time and effort, the benefits are accomplishment, joy, happiness, and triumph.

Neuroscientist have developed brain-reading headphones that can tell when you need a break. The headset can also turn up its noise-cancelling function if it senses you are being distracted. There are sensors in each ear pad that detect the electrical signals in the brain, so it can send the data back via Bluetooth to a smartphone app. They can turn your smartphone notifications off too, to "minimize distractions" when someone is "in the zone." The brain-computer interface headphones have been developed by US firm Neurable. Users will be told when they need a break and what times of the day they seem to be most productive.

Neuroscience will continue to discover how the brain functions, and inventors will continue to develop useful items to enhance our ability to optimize our use of the brain in a most effective way. We are just at the beginning of such innovations and breakthroughs.

## Flow

Flow is a psychological and physiological state of peak performance. It's where we feel our best and perform at our best—both mentally and physically. Some people refer to flow as "being in the zone," "hyper focus," or "full immersion." During flow, mental and physical ability soar, and the brain takes in more information per second, processing it more deeply. During flow, your mind is multiple times more effective. The more time a person spends in flow the greater the increase in productivity which occurs at an astonishing rate. Flow allows you to be more productive, create higher-quality work, and complete your tasks much faster. When you utilize flow states, you do not need to work harder or longer because you're working smarter.

It is that state in which you are at one with an activity or challenge, and nothing else seems to occupy your mind. Your sense of time gets distorted, you are deeply concentrated in the "now," and feelings of hunger, pain, or fatigue might even fade away. Research has shown that, in a flow state, your brainwave activity measurably changes. Brain waves are electrical readings that measure activity. The most commonly measured brainwaves are Delta, Theta, Alpha, and Beta due to existing technology. Gamma waves are prevalent while processing information and learning at a high level. During Gamma, you experience high energy and high focus. Each wave type indicates a level of activity that is occurring in the brain. Delta waves are the slowest and reflect very deep sleep. Theta waves occur when we are meditating or at the initial stage of falling asleep. Theta waves allow our creativity to connect our intuition with our subconscious mind. We can get there naturally by being drowsy or intentionally through skillful meditation. This promotes creativity. Some of our best ideas come to us in this state. Alpha waves are next on the spectrum and usually occur when we relax through proper breathing and meditation. Alpha waves open the door for us to be "in the zone." We can intentionally get into the zone with training. Artists and high-performing athletes train to reach this state of brain waves. The brain shifts from high Beta wave activity (normal, waking consciousness) to the slower waves on the Alpha/Theta borderline.

During Alpha waves (8 to 12 Hz), the brain is calm yet alert. This is where new information is absorbed efficiently and you are fully focused on the "now." This state is usually accessed through meditation. This is akin to daydreaming or creativity, but you are still awake.

During Theta waves (3 to 8 Hz), the brain is in a "dream" state—that zone between being awake and asleep. When in Theta waves, optimal learning, memory, and intuition takes place. This state can also be accessed through deep meditation. Deep thinking also occurs at the wave level.

When we are fully in the zone Gamma waves are prevalent and put us in a state of mind to see reality quicker and process thoughts faster. In complex situations where speed and accuracy are required. This is how high performance is achieved. It is also when a person uses all aspects of the brain, not just part of the brain. Since we can control our thoughts and since our mind controls our body, we can, with proper training, enter any state of mind with a selected brain wave activity.

Aside from changes in brain wave activity, flow also produces a potent shift in neurochemistry. It appears that during a flow state, a combination of brain chemicals is secreted simultaneously. And flow is one of the only times the brain produces them simultaneously. The mental state of flow is pleasurable, meaningful, and a much sought-after state of mind. What state of mind are you in right now?

A deep focus or flow state requires a lot of mental energy. On top of the information overload and abundance of distractions, so little time is spent in a flow state because operating at maximum mental capacity is energy-draining. Therefore, it is critical to do your flow state work when your mental energy levels are at their peak. For most people, this would be early in the day, but since everyone is unique, it could be at other times for you.

There are multiple approaches to get into a flow state of work. Certainly, training and breathing will assist in getting physically ready to enter a flow state of work. One of the main triggers to reach a flow state is your breath. A breathing practice will allow you to reach full concentration, helping you to enter the flow state. The US Special Operations Forces teach techniques such as box breathing because it calms the mind and accelerates the entry into a flow state. Boxed breathing is a deep breathing exercise. Though it may feel unnatural to breathe deeply, the practice comes with various benefits and can be exercised at will in any circumstance. Deep breaths are more efficient: they allow your body to fully exchange incoming oxygen with outgoing carbon dioxide. They have also been shown to slow the heartbeat, lower or stabilize blood pressure, and lower stress. Boxed breathing, also known as four-square breathing, involves exhaling to a count of four, holding your lungs empty for a four-count, inhaling at the same pace, and holding air in your lungs for a count of four before exhaling and beginning the pattern anew. Once in a flow state, the mind is more efficient and is capable of being fully engaged in the task at hand to experience a loss of self-consciousness and a sense of complete mastery of the performance.

Since not everyone is doing physical work such as a professional athlete, there are several considerations to get into and maintain a state or flow work.

Once a decision is made to enter a flow state with a clear

purpose, begin by choosing a quiet and comfortable workspace that is as noise-free as possible. Next, silence all electronic notifications and devices that you will be tempted to check on out of habit and that would interrupt you with push notifications. Depending upon how long you intend to work in the flow state, you may want to prepare a snack and appropriate drink and announce to people that you need silence and freedom from personal interruption while doing this work. Begin with breathing deeply, calming your mind and relaxing your body before entering the flow state. Be comfortable, and keep a clear, sharp mind while working. Keep in mind that it is important to know your optimal time with mental clarity and energy as well as letting your brain take over to do its work. Optimum is neither maximum nor minimum. It is just the right amount of time that is best for each individual. With proper training and regular practice, you can enter the flow state at will.

Consider the case of a basketball great by the name of Stephen Curry of the Golden State Warriors basketball team. His physical size is barely adequate for the National Basketball Association with a height of 6'3" and a weight of 190 pounds. Also, he is not a formidable presence like LeBron James, and he cannot jump like Michael Jordan once did. Yet Curry became the first ever unanimous league MVP in 2016, after also winning the award the previous year and leading his team to win the NBA Championship.

The secret is not just Curry's almost supernatural three-point shooting ability; It is also his ability (as a relatively small guy) to see opportunities for shots on a court filled with giants. Curry specifically trains his perceptive powers, otherwise known as "neurocognitive efficiency" to increase his ability to process sensory input, even at the top of a sport dominated by elites. That means he is seeing more of the game, allowing him to exploit opponents' positioning to create shots, find passing lanes, and force turnovers. Brandon Payne, founder of *Accelerate Basketball* coaches Curry to practice training his perceptive abilities to increase his neurocognitive efficiency. This has helped make his ball-handling crisper and has boosted his creativity, giving him a better command of space on the floor. As a result, when he is in a game, with many variables occurring quickly he must make quick decisions for maximum performance. He follows a regimen that involves "neurological drills" combining simulated game situations with technical dribbling moves. A concentrated overload of all these scenarios during workouts prepares him to mentally slow down the game in real life. It helps him become a smarter basketball player. Payne has personally trained over 100 NBA, WNBA, and foreign professional athletes, including 3x NBA champion and 2x MVP Stephen Curry.

As of June 16, 2022, Stephen Curry was named an NBA Finals M.V.P. after his team, the Golden State Warriors, won the NBA World Championship. His team now has four N.B.A championships, Stephen has two Most Valuable Player Awards and now a Finals M.V.P. award. This illustrates the power of neurocognitive efficiency training combined with effective use of physical abilities, and exercising will power.

Practiced daily, you can rewire the brain to operate from a calmer state all the time. Peak performance is the ability to effortlessly function at your best and is characterized by optimal emotional and cognitive states that include feelings of confidence, focused attention, and clear thinking. To achieve ultimate peak performance, your physical health as well as your emotional and cognitive functions need to be working at an integrated optimal level so you can successfully achieve your goals.

A peak performer is successful in learning throughout their life span. It means that a person is willing, motivated, and able to learn through experiences and changes. Peak performers strive to maintain the right attitude and skills that are needed to reach their goals.

Also consider the case of Tom Brady, an NFL quarterback who at the end of the 2021 NFL season has won seven Super Bowl championships out of ten Super Bowl appearances and is the oldest quarterback on record to date. Brady also uses neuroscience to train his body into forming new habits through a process called neural priming. Brady believes in neuroscience and uses it to create stronger, faster connections in his brain by practicing a habit skill or behavior repeatedly. The more we practice a habit, skill, or behavior, the more automatically our brains recognize it.

In his book *TB12 Method*, Tom Brady describes "how to do what you love, better and for longer."[3] TB12 teamed up with BrainHQ a unique company in the brain-training field for its dedication to the advancement of brain science. In January 30, 2019 Richard Harris, Ap Developers Magazine, explains that the brain training team is led by Dr. Michael Merzenich, who is credited with discovering lifelong plasticity, with being the first to harness plasticity for human benefit (in his co-invention of the cochlear implant), and for pioneering the field of plasticity-based computerized brain exercise. Dr. Merzenich is Professor Emeritus at UCSF and a winner of the Kavli Prize in Neuroscience (the highest honor in the field). He also is the co-founder and Chief Scientific Officer of Posit Science, a company he cofounded to get the latest advances in brain training out of the lab and into the hands of people they could help. Those exercises are available in the training program BrainHQ from Posit Science.

More than one hundred peer-reviewed studies have been published on the technology found in TB12 BrainHQ, showing benefits across varied populations in standard measures of cognition (e.g., speed, attention, memory, and executive function) and generalization to real-world activities (e.g., balance, gait, driving, and everyday cognition). Studies also have shown that exercises in TB12 BrainHQ drive changes in brain chemistry and structure —a demonstration of their use of the brain's natural plasticity. Brady retired from the NFL after the 2021 season and has been described as the greatest quarterback to date in the NFL with impressive records. But wait, there's more. In 2022, Brady announced he is coming out of retirement to play the 2022 NFL season with the Tampa Bay Buccaneers.

What about Simone Biles, the record-holding world class gymnast? Biles is the gymnast with the most World medals (twenty-five) and most World gold medals (nineteen), having surpassed Vitaly Scherbo's record twenty-three World medals by winning her twenty-fourth and twenty-fifth, both golds, at the 2019 competition in Stuttgart. She is the female gymnast with the most World all-around titles (five). Biles is the sixth woman to win an individual all-around title at both the World Championships and the Olympics, and the first gymnast since Lilia Podkopayeva in 1996 to hold both titles simultaneously. Biles is the tenth female gymnast and first US female gymnast to win a World medal on every event, and the first female gymnast since Daniela Silivaș in 1988 to win a medal on every event at a single Olympic Games or World Championships, having accomplished this feat at the 2018 World Championships in Doha.

At the 2020 Summer Olympics in Tokyo, she won the bronze medal on balance beam as well as the silver medal with the US team after struggling with "the twisties," a temporary loss of air balance awareness. Her partial withdrawal, focus on safety, mental health, and perseverance were praised. She temporarily withdrew from competition and went to a secret gym in Tokyo to refocus and retrain her mental discipline to overcome the "twisties" and to again succeed in her physical competition due to her superior mental training and retraining. After the retraining, she won the bronze medal to break her overall medal total on the balance beam.

These high-performing individuals all focus on their mental health and training using extraordinary training techniques that are available to anyone seeking to become a Power Thinker. Power Thinking and training lead to the discovery of previously unknown accomplishments. While we may not all aspire to athletic greatness, by engaging our mental capacity to utilize our most-prized possession, our mind, we can accomplish equally remarkable things in our chosen endeavors. We all are created to own our ability to think and to use our minds for accomplishment.

## Active Recovery for Your Brain

Your mind performs better with a little active recovery. Brain is a part of the body and needs rest even though the subconscious part of our brain is always at work. We have the conscious mind, unconscious mind, and subconscious mind. Even though we are resting the brain, we still engage the brain in a more restorative way. Mental fatigue makes you less efficient and more distractible, irritable, and error-prone. Brain drain affects the whole body. Remember, the brain is to the body what the mind is to the soul. A brain change such as new sights, sounds, smells, or activities can give the brain the rest that it needs. Intense focus for an extended period can cause brain drain. A change of stimuli creates different thoughts and releases different brain chemicals such as dopamine, the pleasure chemical. Our brains respond to something novel and new. Meditation is a form of brain rest. Humor is also a form of brain rest. It has been said that laughter is the best medicine. It is not necessary to laugh on an extended basis, but short burst of laughter can be refreshing.

The Cleveland Clinic in a June 2, 2020 article on mental health entitled "Why Downtime is Essential for Brain Health" suggests that we should give our brain a break. This health and wellness tip helps us keep in mind that it is not healthy for the brain to work extended hours and always stress about unanswered emails or the to-do list. Brain work consumes energy in the body much like physical exercise depletes energy. Nor is it healthy to check the news, the stock market, binge watch a favorite series, or post to social media when the brain needs rest. Detachment from what caused the fatigue is necessary on a periodic basis. This is where unconscious daydreaming is a form of recovery from focus fatigue. It is healthy to weave in appropriate doses of the conscious focus with periodic rests of unconscious non-focus time.

Just like a physical workout is usually comprised of intense sets with periods of rest to build strength, the same thing is important for the brain to have periods of rest to build mental strength. This is akin to mental housekeeping, clearing space for a reset of focused consciousness. This is where positive constructive daydreaming is valuable. It is during this mind "wandering" that mind "wondering" sometimes produces new creative ideas that would not have been possible with cognitive focus and attention for an extended basis. It's like asking ourselves the following question, "What could I be thinking if I wasn't thinking about ....?" These "wonderings" give the prefrontal cortex portion of the brain a proper rest. It could include physical activity such as a stroll in nature, swinging in a hammock, just letting your "unfocused" network come out to frolic. Even a small nap during the work period can revive and rejuvenate the brain as well as the rest of the body to return to a higher productive, rested state for greater productivity. Working memory is rejuvenated during these periods.

According to New York Times author Dave Phillips in his October 1, 2020 article, the US Army has after 70 years revised its fitness field training which was rebranded as the FM 7-22 Holistic Health and Fitness manual. Due to modern neuroscience, even the US Army recognizes this, and, in its updated physical fitness training field manual, it has a new section on napping, which encourages soldiers to use short naps to restore wakefulness and promote performance.

---

## Chapter 3 Summary:
## How to Use Your Brain for Powerful Change

THE LAW of Use and Disuse is also true for the brain. Anything that is not used properly will atrophy or spoil. One of the most important parts of our body is the brain. Under normal circumstances, an aged person still has the use of their brain but perhaps can no longer walk without assistance, even if they were a star athlete in their youth. Our brain is where our mind functions. The physical brain needs oxygen and proper nutrition to optimize the electrical circuits and the chemical releases that we discussed in Chapter 1.

Your brain can learn and grow as you age—a process called brain plasticity—but for it to do so, you must train it on a regular basis. Establishing a routine for proper rest and meditation is important for brain health. Taking up a new activity in the arts or a new physical sport can also improve brain health. Extensive research has found that creative outlets like painting and other art forms, learning an instrument, expressive or autobiographical writing, and learning a language also can improve cognitive function. According to the Harvard Health Publishing of the Harvard Medical School, a 2014 study in Gerontologist reviewed thirty-one studies that focused on how these specific endeavors affected older adults' mental skills and found that all of them improved several aspects of memory like recalling instructions and processing speed. This was reported February 15, 2021 in the Mind and Mood section as "Train Your Brain, Practicing a new and challenging activity is a good bet for building and maintaining cognitive skills".

Whether you are twenty years old or eighty years old, taking care of your physical brain and exercising your mind is critical for a fulfilling and fruitful life. Also, at any age, we still live in a world of volatility, uncertainty, complexity, and ambiguity. We must be our own first responder to the challenges of life. We can employ proper breathing techniques to keep our awareness so we can employ OODA Loop strategies for observation, orientation, decision-making and action when the unexpected occurs in our VUCA world. We should always expect the unexpected and do our own thinking in every situation.

At any age we can effectively use our brain. We can take time to do breathing exercises in addition to the involuntary breathing done by our limbic brain. When there is something that we really want to do, we can exercise our brain to get into a flow state where our senses are heightened, and we can focus on notable events. We can schedule times to let our mind wander to reminisce or imagine new things to think about, to unlock our brain, to discover yet unknown things. How you use your brain is up to you. Become a Power Thinker and a thought leader. You will always be glad you have the use of your brain and thought power.

# 4

## USING POWER THINKING FOR PROBLEM IDENTIFICATION, PRIORITIZATION, AND POWER SOLUTIONS

*Imagination is more important than knowledge, for while knowledge defines everything we know and understand, imagination points to all we might yet discover and create.*

— ALBERT EINSTEIN

A mode of thinking is an approach to thinking. Think about the following story and see if you can identify the thinking mode of the class and the thinking mode of the professor. Also give thought to your own mode of thinking as you read it. The story was written by Marc Chernoff, and was posted June 27, 2019, by PeriodBuddy as a rewritten short story that will change the way you think.

Once upon a time a psychology professor walked around on a stage while teaching stress management principles to an auditorium filled with students. As she raised a glass of water, everyone expected they'd be asked the typical "glass half empty or glass half full" question. Instead, with a smile on her face, the professor asked, "How heavy is this glass of water I'm holding?" Students shouted out answers ranging from eight ounces to a couple pounds.

She replied, "From my perspective, the absolute weight of this glass doesn't matter. It all depends on how long I hold it. If I hold it for a minute or two, it's fairly light. If I hold it for an hour straight, its weight might make my arm ache a little. If I hold it for a day straight, my arm will likely cramp up and feel completely numb and paralyzed, forcing me to drop the glass to the floor. In each case, the weight of the glass doesn't change, but the longer I hold it, the heavier it feels to me."

As the class nodded their heads in agreement, she continued, "Your stresses and worries in life are very much like this glass of water. Think about them for a while and nothing happens. Think about them a bit longer and you begin to ache a little. Think about them all day long, and you will feel completely numb and paralyzed—incapable of doing anything else until you drop them."[1]

Learn to become self-aware of your thinking mode and learn to shift modes. Start with reflection questions such as asking yourself, "What mode have I been thinking in lately?" Next, ask yourself, "What mode of thinking do I want to use to accomplish what I want?" Afterall, the one thing that you have total control over is your thinking. Choose the mode of thinking that makes you feel better and that will let you have an attitude of gratitude. As Zig Ziglar, motivational speaker and author of *See You at the Top says* "Your attitude, not your aptitude, will determine your altitude."[2]

There are a variety of modes of thinking. A mode of thinking is a way in which a person tends to think based on experience, beliefs, learning, and reason. There are different modes of thinking. Most people have a dominant mode of thinking. Being aware of your mode or your go-to mode is a first step in directing your thoughts to consider shifting from your current thoughts and begin thinking first of what you are grateful for and then what you would like to do or have. Modes and models of thinking should be interesting and fun. Have fun exploring all modes and many models of thinking to find your next ideas to put into action.

Here are a few modes of thinking for you to consider:

**Focused Mode:** When you are concentrating on something, be it shooting a ball or solving a math problem, your brain operates in the focused mode.

**Defeatist Mode:** This mental state is dominated by worry, frustration, and fear of what might go wrong.

**Sustainer Mode:** In this state of mind, we're mostly "going through the motions," sustaining the status quo. We incessantly check our devices. We multitask, and we grind it out—on autopilot.

**Dreamer Mode:** If this is your mental state at present, give your brain a kiss! You're on a performance path, at least as far as generating ideas is concerned. Something has stimulated these endorphins of possibility, and it's important to identify what.

**Opportunity Mode:** In this mode, our idea factories are operating at peak performance levels. Opportunity mode builds upon the dreamer mode, but there's an added element: an action-taking component. You are not content just to hatch ideas—you have intention to make those dreams a reality.

**Diffuse Mode:** This is all about making subconscious and unconscious connections in your brain, allowing the understanding of new and abstract concepts, as well as the approach of a problem from different angles. Due to this free "movement" in the brain, the diffuse mode focuses on the breadth of thoughts and neural connections rather than the depth. We do this when we let our mind wander so it can wonder.

### Develop Clear Thinking: Remodel, Re-mode, Reload

*Remodel*

Remodeling is a common practice when a person wants to change the structure or form of something. Typically, one thinks of remodeling a building or room or some physical structure. In Power Thinking, one thinks about changing the structure or form of thoughts or ways of thinking to shape them again or differently. Futurist Alvin Toffler in his 1970 book *Future Shock* is attributed as saying, "The illiterate of the 21st century will not be those who cannot read and write, but those who cannot learn, unlearn, and relearn."[3]

Mental models are a set of beliefs and ideas that we consciously or unconsciously form based on our experiences. They guide our thoughts and behaviors and help us develop an understanding of the thing we are thinking about. Mental models are just thinking tools for efficient reasoning. There are many mental models that are developed and employed, and they lead to many mindsets. The key aspect of finding or developing a mental model is to examine the reason behind the model. Asking a lot of questions unlocks learning. The quality of the question determines the quality of the answer. Therefore, avoid trivial questions with shallow meanings. Give careful consideration as to the why behind the question. Is the why a simple curiosity to explain an urge, or is it a deep burning desire to understand something deeply?

Ness Labs, a group of curious thinkers who encourage a person to build a lab for their mind with neuroscience-based content and conversations, offers the following tips you can apply to master mental models rather than being enslaved by them:

1. Be aware of your thinking by asking yourself provocative questions.
2. Gather information to challenge your thinking with actual facts.
3. Inquire into other people's thinking and challenge their views.
4. Resist jumping to conclusions and suspend your assumptions.
5. Look for recurring thought patterns and unlearn them.

A tool is only as good as its user. However, once you're aware of your mental models, you can use them effectively to achieve your goals. Therefore, dedicate yourself to mindful productivity.

## Re-mode

As mentioned earlier, a mode of thinking is based upon experience and reason. Here we will investigate Motivation and Opportunity as Determinants through Exploration (MODE) theory, which is one of many explanations for human behavior. MODE theory says that the extent to which an attitude will affect our behaviors as human beings will differ depending on the amount of deliberation before an act is committed. MODE theory was first proposed by US psychologist Russell H Fazio. His work focuses on social psychological phenomena like attitude formation and change, the relationship between attitudes and behavior, and the automatic and controlled cognitive processes that guide social behavior. We have previously examined that an attitude is a habit of thought. Habits are formed by repeating a thought that initiates a repeated action. In our brain when we have a new thought it may just be a one-time thing that is stored in short term memory. However, when it is repeated multiple times, a neural pathway is established in working memory and with continued repetitions our brain establishes the thought and the action in long term memory via a new neural pathway. When the thought trigger leads to a predictable action the brain uses little energy in the automatic response and we do it without really thinking much about it. Therefore, care must be exercised to establish and maintain the right habits of thought.

When we "re-mode" our thinking, we reconsider our motivation behind something. Motivation is a motive for action. Have our motives changed? Are our opportunities the same, different, or no longer present? What are we now determining to focus our thinking on? Are we ready to reaffirm our motivation to recognize an opportunity and determine or redetermine a continuance of the actions for which we have been motivated? Have things changed so that we must identify new opportunities, change our determinants, and apply new emotional energy to think and act on something different? What must we relearn or unlearn? What else can we explore?

"Re-moding" our thinking causes us to explore and examine new and different opportunities that may motivate us to decide to do something different or to reaffirm that we are already doing what we are motivated to do.

## Reload

After having reshaped our thoughts, to reaffirm or form new goals to achieve our mission, on the journey of our vision to fulfill our purpose, new goals, strategies, and tactics may be timely. When an idea presents itself, back it up with immediate action. We then reload our routines and disciplines to accomplish what we desire.

George Scialabba, American Essayist and Critic said, "Creativity is intelligence having fun." So, let's have fun exploring the three prominent modes of thinking: convergent thinking, divergent thinking, and lateral thinking.[4]

## Convergent Thinking

When faced with a problem, convergent thinking is an effective way to find the best possible solution from a wide array of possibilities. This mode of thinking leads to solutions by using known criteria to transform ideas into actionable steps. Convergent thinking, a term created by Joy Paul Guilford in his book *The Nature of Human Intelligence*, focuses on finding the single, correct solution to any problem by following defined, logical steps. With convergent thinking, answers are either right or wrong, with zero ambiguity.[5] Convergent thinking can narrow down large numbers of possible solutions by analyzing all possible options logically. It helps you find the very best solution by comparing each possibility against real-world constraints and established criteria.

Convergent thinking is also known as critical, vertical, analytical, or linear thinking. Convergent thinking pulls all known facts together and examines them logically to find the best final answer. The main goal of convergent thinking is finding a single, provable solution to any problem. This mode of thinking emphasizes speed, logic, and accuracy.

### Divergent Thinking

Divergent thinking is on the opposite end of the scale of convergent thinking. While convergent thinking is looking for just one solution, divergent thinking is considering many possible solutions. Divergent thinking is a thought process or method used to generate creative ideas by exploring many possible solutions. It typically occurs in a spontaneous, free flowing, nonlinear manner. Divergent thinking produces many ideas which are generated in an emergent cognitive fashion during a divergent thinking exercise.

Divergent thinking is the capacity to find relationships between ideas, concepts, and processes that, at first glance, lack any similarity. All of us, regardless of age, can practice and improve our divergent thinking. Divergent thinking involves the following four skills:

1. Fluency: the ability to produce many ideas
2. Flexibility: the ability to create a wide variety of ideas based on different fields of knowledge
3. Originality: the ability to create innovative ideas
4. Development: the ability to improve our ideas, to make them more sophisticated

Many possible solutions are explored in a short amount of time, and unexpected connections are drawn. Divergent thinking is involved in lateral thinking because divergent thinking creates many possibilities. Lateral thinking is not just concerned with generating alternatives but also with changing patterns and switching to new and better patterns. Divergent thinking goes together with joy, optimism, and inner well-being. Divergent thinking can enjoy a dopamine rush. Having good relationships, being well-rested, and being free of pressure, anxiety, and stress puts you in an ideal position for divergent thinking. This also releases other happy chemicals in the brain. With our high-pressure, busy lives, we neglect many of these valuable dimensions.

## Lateral Thinking

When using lateral thinking, the individual needs to be able to see the right answer that convergent thought would create. A lateral thinker can also see the divergent answers. They not only look at the right solution or the what-if solution but also pull them all together.

The basic theoretical premise behind lateral thinking is known as pattern changing. People love to look for and follow patterns because they are predictable and sometimes explainable, and therefore comforting as a result. Our mind loves to find connections between things, even if they aren't really there.

But lateral thinking is all about changing patterns. Instead of looking at some sort of pattern and then moving forward with that pattern, step by step, lateral thinking either restructures old patterns or comes up with completely new ideas altogether.

Another important premise behind lateral thinking is attitude. Attitudes are habits of thought. Lateral thinking is as much about restructuring our attitudes as it is about changing old patterns. A good lateral thinking attitude is accepting that patterned ways of looking at things or doing things can be useful; it's not about disregarding them outright. However, lateral thinking is also about having the attitude that an old, structured way isn't necessarily an absolute, nor is it necessarily unique. In other words, other (potentially better) alternatives may be possible. That's the mindset of a lateral thinker!

Another critical aspect of the theory behind lateral thinking is forward thinking. Lateral thinking is not about the analysis of the events that led up to the current point in order to figure out if the current point is where you want to be. Lateral thinkers do not look back to justify what has led them to where they are. Instead, they look forward. Instead of analyzing a past event, they focus on the information they have in hand and the effect this information may have in determining a future outcome.

Within each mode of thinking, there are one or more models of thinking. A model of thinking is a set of beliefs and ideas that we consciously or unconsciously form based on our experiences. Thinking models are created frameworks to use while thinking about something that we want to explore.

A person's usual mindset should be suspended while going through a particular mode of thinking because in Power Thinking, one must keep an open mind for discovery. Again, depending upon the thinking task, consider what mode you should use before you try one or more modes of thinking to see how your thoughts differ and why you think there are additional insights to consider.

The first step is to identify the focus of your thinking in a particular context or setting. Do you want to think about the big picture on a macro level or a detailed picture on the micro level? This will assist you in determining what mode to use.

At the macro or big picture level, depending upon your thinking style, you may consider thinking about generating creative ideas, designing effective systems, mobilizing people into action, or building and strengthening relationships. These are usually macro big picture things. At the micro or detailed level, you may consider thinking about achieving objectivity and insight. You may also think about improving productivity and efficiency. Or at this level you could be thinking about achieving completion and momentum on a project. If you are engaging one or more team members in an organization, you might think about cultivating people and potential.

Convergent thinking and divergent thinking can be likened to a certain lens. For example, a convex lens faces outward more like an ever-expanding bigger picture. This lens is like divergent thinking which looks at the big picture. This would be like zooming out a camera lens for the largest landscape picture. Conversely by zooming in the camera lens to find the smallest detail, a concave lens is employed. A concave lens faces inward like a smaller picture. That is like convergent thinking. Thinking can be done by converging on critical and analytical types of thought which are looking for or looking to verify an answer to a thought experiment designed to find a finite solution. This would be using a concave lens to bring things to a fine point. Another way to express this is to engage in vertical thinking or directional thinking. Divergent thoughts like the convex lens looks to expand to the big picture and can expand horizontally in both directions by using the imagination in a creative thought exercise.

A quantum thinking model would consider doing both at the same time to contrast and compare the results. This would be using both convergent and divergent thinking on the same area of focus. Lateral thinking can look for patterns to maintain, or change, depending upon the problem that needs to be solved. Lateral thinking is an application of the quantum thinking model which considers two things as being possible at the same time.

## Models of Thinking

Models of thinking are just various approaches to consider how to think about something. Different models of thinking are best suited for different situations.

## Mental Thinking Models

A mental model is an explanation of how something works. The phrase "mental model" is an overarching term for any sort of concept, framework, or worldview that you carry around in your mind.

Mental models help you understand life. Mental models also guide your perception and behavior. They are the thinking tools that you use to understand life, make decisions, and solve problems. Learning a new mental model gives you a new way to see the world.

Mental models are imperfect but useful. There is no single mental model which provides a flawless explanation of anything, however we must create a model to guide our thought process that fits what we are investigating.

## Design Thinking

Design thinking is an innovative problem-solving process rooted in a set of skills. Design thinking is like ambidextrous thinking by thinking from both sides of an issue. It considers disruptive technology and looks at the macro-view by designing systems for success while considering the micro view of the persons involved or effected by the design. Design thinking relies on our ability: to be intuitive, to recognize patterns, and to construct ideas that have emotional meaning as well as functionality. It allows us to express ourselves in media other than words or symbols. It is the integration of intuition and inspiration with what is rational and analytic. Design thinking encourages us to explore different possibilities. Applying a designer's sensibility and methods to problem solving helps us to develop a deep understanding of the consumer based on fieldwork research using an ethnographic approach and methods by watching, listening, discussing, and seeking to understand by considering different points of view. Design thinking is not seeking persuasion. However, it can accelerate learning through visualization, hands-on experimentalism, and creating quick prototypes, which are made as simple as possible in order to get usable feedback. Design thinking is focused more on radical than on incremental innovation. Use design thinking when big issues need new ways of thinking.

## First Principles Thinking

First principles thinking drives complex problem-solving and workplace innovation through reverse engineering. Individuals and organizations that employ first principles thinking are one step ahead as they plan and build for the future.

We start with multiple principles in life governed by our values, perceptions, belief system and how we learn to reason. These principles lead to opinions and gives leeway to our brain to apply shortcuts in the form of conclusions it learned before.

We learn to live with them without validating the underlying assumptions. The principles may be sound when we first start, but questioning if they still apply requires debunking old theories and creating new versions of reality for ourselves.

First principles thinking requires embracing a new mindset that identifies when our old way of doing things is obsolete. A shift in thinking that discards conventional wisdom, cuts through the dogma, and questions our own beliefs.

| Traditional Thinking - How We Typically Think | First Principles Thinking - How We Should Think |
|---|---|
| Starts with limitations | Starts with possibilities |
| Iteration and improvement of an established path | Define and explore a completely new path |
| Explore available solutions in the form of variations of what exists without true knowledge | Create a new recipe from the fundamental truth |
| Look back in time and then determine what to build | Look into the future and its needs |
| Question the path taken to reach a certain goal | Ask the question "What's the goal?" |

First principles thinking (also called reasoning from first principles) requires breaking down a problem into its fundamental building blocks, its essential elements, asking powerful questions, getting down to the basic truth, separating facts from assumptions, and then constructing a view from the grounds up.

It requires understanding that our experience may be different from reality and true knowledge can be attained by learning to integrate different ideas together. It fills the gap between the incremental mindset to opening ourselves to the beautiful world of possibilities. While Elon Musk did not invent the electric vehicle, he used first principles thinking to create the famous electric vehicle company known as Tesla.

## Systems

Systems thinking is a language for learning and acting. It helps us see how we create our reality while pointing to higher leverage solutions to problems. It is a discipline for seeing structures (the patterns and connections) underlying seemingly diverse personal, organizational, and societal issues. A basic system is input, transformation, output, and feedback. Systems involve planning, methods, order, and arrangement. This is the opposite of chaotic. Power Thinkers observe, analyze, design, and activate systems or redesign existing systems. Systems are like gyroscopes in that they guide and control direction. Gyroscopes can be used to provide stability or maintain a reference direction in navigation systems, automatic pilots, and stabilizers. Systems philosophy is a way of thinking about phenomena in terms of wholes, including parts, components, or subsystems, and with emphasis on their interrelationships. Systems analysis is used in problem-solving or decision-making. Decision-making starts with intelligence-gathering and searching for conditions calling for a decision.

Power Thinkers understand the interrelatedness of systems and recognize that some things can be designed to reinforce action and others can be designed to balance the forces at work. Systems thinking and design are important for optimum performance. Famously quoted by the Deming Institute and in his book *Out of the Crisis,* Deming said, "A bad system will beat a good person every time."[6] Deming went on to say that "Eighty-five percent of the reasons for failure are deficiencies in the systems and process rather than the employee. The role of management is to change the process rather than badgering individuals to do better."[7] Power Thinkers and thought leaders examine existing systems to determine whether the current system is promoting success and excellence or if changing conditions necessitate a system redesign. This involves taking the journey from data to wisdom that was mentioned earlier.

## Systems Thinking

A system is a group of interacting, interrelated, or interdependent components that form a complex and unified whole. A systems component can be physical objects that you can touch, or intangible components such as processes, relationships, information flows, interpersonal interaction, and internal states of mind such as feelings, values, and beliefs. Examples of systems that are physical include an automobile, an airplane, and the human body. An intangible example is a mastermind alliance or the mastermind plans in the mind of a Power Thinker.

There are natural systems and there are humanmade systems. Consider the solar system created by God or an ecosystem like the ocean. These have infinite connectivity to other systems. Humanmade systems can be complex, but they are non-thriving systems and are not infinitely connected to systems around them.

Systems thinking offers a set of tools and a framework for looking at issues as systemic wholes. The principles of systems thinking are: thinking of the big picture; balancing short-term and long-term perspectives; recognizing the dynamic, complex, and interdependent nature of systems considering both measurable and non-measurable factors; and remembering that we are all part of the systems in which we function and that we each influence those systems even as we are being influenced by them.

As we seek to uncover systemic structures, we consider

behavior overtime and what is known as a causal loop diagram. In considering behavior overtime, thinkers look for the variables that are affecting our area of focus. One then picks a time frame for the consideration and begins to offer theories about the problem to be solved. Causal loop diagrams are next in the process where one considers such things as feedback loops that are either reinforcing or balancing processes. Next, one considers the relationships between variables and determines if a variable is an engine of growth or a stabilizer. These things contribute to the complexity of understanding the system. There are several mental models that can be discovered in this process.

Use systems thinking to discover rather than to promote an agenda. Use systems thinking to sift out major issues and factors that need to be addressed. Systems thinking should not be employed to find someone to blame, rather use systems thinking to promote inquiry and challenge preconceived ideas. In other words, this is a tool for thinkers, not manipulators.

The best mental models are the ideas with the most utility. They are broadly useful in daily life. Understanding these concepts will help you make wiser choices and take better actions. Therefore, developing a broad base of mental models is critical for anyone interested in thinking clearly, rationally, and effectively. Here are some additional mental models to consider:

**Model 1:** Address the important, ignore the urgent (the Eisenhower model). Observe what is truly important and ignore "noisy" non-factors. Black Swan events, equilibrium points, and regression to the mean all obscure our thoughts because they are more emotional than realistic. Emotions may not be trustworthy. The emotions are not always subject to reason, but they are always subject to action.

**Model 2:** Visualize all the dominoes to make a well-informed decision. If you have ever lined up a set of dominoes and then started the first one to fall, have a picture of this. However, should just one domino be spaced farther apart from the length of a domino, the falling dominoes stop, and the rest are left standing. Therefore, it is important to consider multiple impacts. Mindfulness is your mind's eye. So, what lenses do you choose? Sparring with a different mind's eye allows you to see things differently. This synergy results in an incredible mind meld, which enriches each mind's eye. This also works like a mastermind alliance. Consider different mind's eyes. For example, Warren Buffet has an investor's eye while Bill Gates has a technologist's eye. What eye do you have? What would it be like to think about different things in different ways?

Curiosity is what pushes both to always find out more, and focus is what lets both achieve results. When you use a mental model to identify something or try to predict what will happen, when it doesn't happen or can't be identified, ask the question, "What about my mental model that is wrong?" followed by the question, "Where can I learn more?"

**Model 3:** Make reversible decisions with an action bias. Use a growth mindset process. Reversible decisions are doors that open both ways. Irreversible decisions are doors that allow passage in only one direction; if you walk through, you are stuck there. Most decisions are the former and can be reversed (even though we can never recover the invested time and resources). Many decisions are reversible, i.e., two-way doors.

Some decisions are consequential and irreversible or nearly irreversible—one-way doors—and these decisions must be made methodically, carefully, slowly, with great deliberation and consultation. Give careful consideration backup and emergency plans in case of unforeseen circumstances. Consider alternative procedures if once you go through the irreversible door, you discover a problem. If you walk through and don't like what you see on the other side, you can't get back to where you were before. But most decisions aren't like that—they are changeable, reversible—they're two-way doors. If you've made a suboptimal two-way door decision, you don't have to live with the consequences for that long. You can reopen the door and go back through. The next time you struggle to decide, first determine the consequences.

**Model 4:** Seek "satisfiction" (fictional satisfaction) a term that blends an idea that would perhaps both satisfy and suffice as a solution. No need to become paralyzed by seeking perfection. Immense curiosity and the ability to focus. Perfection is rarely achieved. Therefore, consider what would be the minimal level of satisfaction to be "satisfiction."

**Model 5:** Stay within 40 percent to 70 percent of the available information for a quick decision. Think fast, learn fast. There are two levels of thinking here. One is the quick intuition model of thinking, which is many times a good decision. Another level considers Bloom's Taxonomy approach where one gathers knowledge, considers whether it is the correct thing, and also considers other things. Next, test this by putting it to use, then analyze the result of this thing as you consider putting various parts together to make something. Then evaluate the results. This is the major contrast between quick thinking based on intuition and slow thinking based on a more considered approach. This model is a "think fast" model.

**Model 6:** Minimize regret by projecting forward and looking back from that projection. Prepare your mind for action. Be sober-minded, alert, keep your wits about you. Be self-controlled. Do not be conformed but be transformed. Follow the truth with a pure heart. There is power in each of us to learn and change, to be transformed.

A mindset of dreams and imaginations with no fences or boundaries is the cousin to creativity, so allow it to go beyond what is expected to experience what you have not seen before. It feeds off the fact that there is always a better way and feeds a creative mind that allows you to realize that there is always a way to see, do, feel, and think creatively. This takes you from the world you live in to the one you could live in. Only by imagination can things first start to be accomplished, so let it go and see for yourself.

**Model 7:** Inversion thinking. This way of thinking, in which you consider the opposite of what you want, is known as inversion. It is a powerful thinking model. Inversion is a rare and crucial skill that nearly all great thinkers use to their advantage. Inversion is a powerful thinking tool because it puts a spotlight on errors and roadblocks that are not obvious at first glance. What if the opposite was true? What if I focused on a different side of this situation? Instead of asking how to do something, ask how to not do it. Great thinkers, icons, and innovators think forward and backward. They consider the opposite side of things. Occasionally, they drive their brain in reverse. This way of thinking can reveal compelling opportunities for innovation. You can learn just as much from identifying what doesn't work as you can from spotting what does. What are the mistakes, errors, and flubs that you want to avoid? Inversion is not about finding good advice but rather about finding anti-advice. It teaches you what to avoid.

---

### Chapter 4 Summary:
### Using Power Thinking for Problem Identification,
### Prioritization, and Power Solutions

A mode of thinking is an approach to thinking. A diffuse mode is all about making subconscious and unconscious connections in your brain, allowing the understanding of new and abstract concepts, as well as the approach of a problem from different angles. Due to this free "movement" in the brain, the diffuse mode focuses on the breadth of thoughts and neural connections rather than the depth. We do this when we let our mind wander so it can wonder.

Models of thinking are just various approaches to consider how to think about something. Different models of thinking are best suited for different situations. Be creative and develop new models or thought experiments to help you give thought to creating a solution to a perplexing problem or to release your creativity to explore unlimited possibilities.

Your mode (approach to thinking) and the model you choose to use in your thinking can have many permutations and combinations. Permutations and combinations are the ways to represent a group of objects, in this case thoughts, by selecting them in a set and forming subsets. A permutation defines the various ways to arrange a certain group of things, in this case thoughts grouped together. A combination deals with sequence or the order in which they are represented within the set or subset. Sometimes moving a thought from one set to another reveals aspects of the thought that you had not previously considered. Likewise with the order in which they occur in sequence, which sheds new light on the problem you are solving or on the creative imaginative things you had not previously considered. Grouping thoughts together or changing the grouping and the multiple orders of thoughts for each set allows you to see many different aspects of what you are thinking about. Also, changing modes and models within each thought experiment is a good approach to exercise creative reasoning. If you are seeking to be imaginative, you will quickly discover what stimulates additional thoughts and what stifles them. That is why exercising your thought power can be so very rewarding and powerful.

# POWER THINKING TOOLS FOR POWER LEADERSHIP

*Five percent of the people think; ten percent of the people think
they think; and the other eighty-five percent would rather die
than think.*

— THOMAS A. EDISON, INVENTOR

## Deep Thought and Study

One powerful thought that is a condensation of a thought
by Plutarch is "the mind is a fire to be kindled not a
vessel to be filled." One way of kindling the mental fire is by
asking powerful questions. Powerful questions are not the
everyday questions that have easy answers; for example, what is
the forecast for today's weather, or what time does an event start?
Powerful questions are provocative. They kindle creative thinking
that stimulates innovative ideas, which in turn can lead to new

innovations. Powerful questions are usually short and precise with a focus on one idea at a time. A powerful question is easy to remember and is open-ended. This allows cogitation, which is thinking deeply about something, to occur consciously, in a deliberate and intentional way. A powerful question under consideration can also be assigned to the subconscious mind for continual processing. This allows conscious and subconscious thinking to be engaged to give insight as an answer is discovered.

## Quantum Thinking

Quantum thinking is the ability to see an issue from all sides. In general, scientific terms, "quantum" describes an effect that cannot be explained by classical approaches. It has also come to mean an unmeasurable jump in speed or volume. At the quantum level of thinking, one must be able to hold two contradictory states at the same time rather than at the binary state of a yes or a no or of a light switch that is either on or off. At the macro level, it seems that there must be a choice of on or off, but at the micro level it seems to be both at the same time. Consider that if you flip a coin, the outcome will be either heads or tails. But what happens if you spin the coin instead of flipping it? It is both at the same time. And it does not matter if you started the flip with a head up or a tail up, while it is flipping in a spin it could be either or both.

The key is that quantum thought requires you to both agree and disagree with an argument at the same time—to keep yourself in the world of probabilities rather than zeroes and ones with a predictable outcome. This is important not only in the initial stages of research and discovery but also in determining the best solution to a problem or even if you are deciding if you are solving the right problem.

The more complicated the world becomes, the less likely that a simple solution exists. Quantum thinking involves considering more than one hypothesis at the same time. We must be wary of quick answers while we are in the middle of examining the question or a variety of questions.

Quantum thinking allows one to deconstruct, analyze, and test arguments before a conclusion or solution is determined. Many people believe in data-driven decisions, but a quantum thinker would believe in data-informed decisions where judgment, understanding, and wisdom are employed. Data is quantitative, but one must also consider qualitative aspects. Although this quote is attributed to Albert Einstein it was William Bruce Cameron in his book *Informal Sociology, a casual introduction to sociological thinking* , that mentions "not everything that counts can be counted and not everything that can be counted counts." Therefore, avoid being driven by data or any unexamined and untriangulated fact or observation.

Conduct a thought experiment. A thought experiment is a hypothetical situation in which a hypothesis, theory, or principle is laid out for the purpose of thinking through its consequences. Take care to structure it well with clearly defined hypothetical questions of things that may or may not have happened or even will happen. In thought experiments, we gain added information by rearranging or reorganizing already known empirical data in a new way and drawing new (a priori) inferences from them or by looking at these data from a different and unusual perspective. A priori, a Latin phrase means to derive by reasoning while post priori, also a Latin term, presents an observable fact unknowable by reason alone.

Thought experiments have been conducted by such innovators as Elon Musk, who first imagined an electric car company that drives the clean energy movement by virtually all car manufacturers in the twenty-first century. Consider also the thought experiments produced by Steve Jobs, as he pursued the invention and continuous improvement of the Apple iPhone. Apple iPhones have become ubiquitous in their use as a communication device in almost all forms and also serve as a computer, camera, and digital companion. Who would have thought? There are many examples of individuals who first conducted thought experiments and then brought innovative ideas to reality.

Questions beget thinking; therefore, asking powerful questions can lead to powerful thinking. Asking powerful questions can provide powerful answers. But what are powerful questions? Powerful questions provoke creative thinking that leads to innovative ideas, which in turn lead to innovation. Powerful questions cause us to think deeply. To begin, examine the purpose of the thinking exercise; however, this could lead to several purposes. Keep the question short and precise. This makes it easy to remember and makes it easily understandable. The most important thing, though, is that it is clear. Examples include:

- What will be the impact of…?
- What are the barriers to…?
- Is there another way?
- What's hard right now?
- What's making it difficult to stick to my…?
- What are my obstacles in…?
- If I had three wishes to change things in my control, what would they be?

Keeping a question open-ended allows the questioning to avoid assumptions and not become a leading question. Write the question down without giving it too much thought. The objective is to stimulate focused thinking without evaluating exact form. Sometimes it helps to reframe the question. This often shifts perspectives and dramatically changes the mental conversations.

Another approach is to reverse brainstorm. Rather than brainstorming what you want, brainstorm the opposite of what you want. This alternative approach can harness negative energy such as cynicism, sarcasm, and hostility to spark creativity. This considers all the things that can be done to make an endeavor not succeed. While this seems ludicrous, looking to accomplish or block accomplishment reveals insight in both directions.

Powerful questions will yield insight that ordinary people miss. Consider the following list of questions:

- What uncertainties should I be worried about?
- What opportunities am I missing?
- What will I have to have less of to achieve more?
- What else am I missing?

Questions like these open the door to the future and are more powerful than answers in that they demand thinking about some things you may not want to think about so that when you think about what you really want to, you have multiple perspectives to guide the authenticity of your thoughts. Asking a lot of questions unlocks learning. Questions and thoughtful answers lead to great discovery. The wellspring of all questions is wonder and curiosity and a capacity for delight when an answer appears.

## Observe

Observation is an important skill. Taking in all items, actions, conditions, and what is happening in sequence means that you must be attentive to the obvious and the not so obvious. Attention to detail is important. This encourages decision-making that has been reviewed by critical thinking, an analysis of possible threats and opportunities, and how to neutralize or capture an opportunity. Observation combined with powerful questions can be very revealing to a Power Thinker.

## Analyze

Think and rethink, but don't overthink. Analysis involves separating things into their parts or an idea into its parts to figure out all the nature and interrelationship of all the parts or to consider and evaluate a situation carefully. Critical thinking is the objective analysis and evaluation of an issue in order to form a judgment. Critical thinking requires you to use your ability to reason. Critical thinkers are active learners rather than passive recipients of information. Critical thinking is thinking about things in certain ways to arrive at the best possible solution in the circumstances that the thinker is aware of. It is a way of thinking about whatever is presently occupying your mind so that you come to the best possible conclusion.

Critical thinkers rigorously question ideas and assumptions rather than accepting them at face value. They will always seek to determine whether the ideas, arguments, and findings represent the entire picture and are open to finding that they do not. In a way, critical thinkers are looking for the who, what, when, where, how, and why behind something. After they have identified the arguments, they evaluate the different viewpoints to recognize the positive or negative ones for evaluating the strengths and weaknesses that are evident. This allows them to provide structured reasoning and support for an argument that we wish to make, not just to make a point but also to aim at achieving the best possible outcome in any situation. It provides a clear assessment of current and possible outcomes. It provides insight and foresight based upon experience and the rational process of analysis and synthesis of intellect and emotions, insights, judgments, assumptions, known truths, and current expected truths.

Synthesis becomes possible by analysis since analysis breaks things down into their simplest parts so that synthesis can create something new, different, or improved. Analysis and synthesis are used by both the arts and science. They lead to creativity. Critical thinkers will identify, analyze, and solve problems systematically rather than by intuition or instinct.

Why does it matter? No one wants to be a fool or play the fool. Therefore, power thinking is tied to wisdom and develops disciplined thought habits. On the journey from data to wisdom, data may be analyzed and synthesized to provide information that, with deeper study, may produce knowledge that develops understanding.

Learning compounds, therefore, as we learn more we can develop a deeper understanding which enables us to act wisely. Learners are thinkers. Thinkers who develop understanding and wisdom for action lead all the followers. Thought leaders who skillfully, consistently, and insightfully observe, consider, imagine, and innovate are the ones who impact and change the world. Power Thinkers and thought leaders bear the fruit of wisdom. You can become a thought leader of thought leaders by getting your Certified Thought Leader credential from the Center for Quality Leadership.

## Atomic Thinking with Fission and Fusion in Atomic Thinking Creativity

Fission is the splitting or breaking up into parts. In nuclear fission, which is the power of the atomic bomb, fission occurs when a neutron slams into a larger atom, forcing it to excite and spilt into two smaller atoms—also known as fission products. Additional neutrons are also released that can initiate a chain reaction, which generates enormous power as energy is released. Not just for bombs, which are destructive, nuclear fission is used in the generation of electricity through nuclear power plants.

Fusion, on the other hand, occurs when two atoms slam together to form a heavier atom, like when two hydrogen atoms fuse to form one helium atom. This is the same process that powers the sun and creates massive amounts of energy—several times greater than fission. It also doesn't produce highly radioactive fission products. While nuclear fusion is being studied to produce energy on earth, it could be possible by the year 2025 or 2026, depending upon which group makes the breakthrough first. Jeff Bezos, founder of Amazon, is funding a Canadian start-up "General Fusion" that uses different metals in generating magnetic fields to create the fusion. This fusion reaction will then transmit heat to surrounding water, which will be converted to steam to drive turbines and create electricity. Other companies are also exploring different methodologies to create nuclear fusion. Organizations like the International Thermonuclear Experimental Reactor (ITER) are working together with countries like the United States, Russia, China, India, Japan, South

Korea, the United Kingdom, and the countries doing business in the European Union to create a device that would develop nuclear fusion.

A Power Thinker can study divergent and convergent ideas within a Master Mind Alliance to break ideas into basic parts with analysis and with synthesis and assemble the parts into new and more innovative and powerful ideas as the fission and fusion of thoughts present themselves. Thinking creates energy, which can be channeled into action. While thoughts are powerful, this application of thought fission or thought fusion is what sparks Power Thinking and brings ideas into existence. The previous explanation of nuclear fission and fusion are results of a Power Thinker putting into the physical equivalent of their thoughts. This application of fusing thoughts together or breaking them into their smallest parts is a means for breakthrough thinking. Breakthroughs occur when we go well beyond current imagined boundaries.

The use of analysis and synthesis allows us to discover voluntary disruption, to change, restore, replace, rethink, and reimagine. Change is really the only constant. Since change is going to happen, why not, as a Power Thinker, lead a positive change before a negative change occurs?

### Solving Deep Problems with Deep Thinking

Deep thinkers use their brains. In our current society, it is easy to be constantly engaged in a digital input and a digital addiction that stifles our creative curiosity due to constant notifications that change our focus. Likewise, patience and wonder are affected by our shortened attention span because of constant bombardment of soundbites, slogans, and thoughts being driven by someone else rather than by ourselves because we are easily distracted. It is like we have overdosed on information that someone else wants to share with us. Certainly, we all want to be part of a tribe, and so we are quick to respond to stimuli from the tribe. This leads us into the echo chamber environment where a person only encounters information or opinions that reflect and reinforce their own. As a result, a person rarely thinks deeply for themselves. Additionally, it is easy to let media outlets steer our thoughts for easy answers. Many people use texting as a means of saving time in communication. Texting allows us to fire off a text and then return to digital addiction from which we were interrupted but we should use thoughtful consideration of the accuracy and impact of the text. When quick response texting happens, we are deprived of our ability to use our God-given power over our thoughts and our intelligence to think differently and deeply.

We can however, reverse this practice and learn how to think differently and deeply and be amazed at our creative and critical thinking skills. Simply put, deep thinking is thinking about thinking. Metacognition is awareness of our thoughts that wonder about our thinking. For example, have you ever wondered about letting your mind wander in curiosity to learn, remember, and think? Another way to look at it is that cognition is thinking to acquire knowledge for understanding. Metacognition helps us be aware of and in control of our cognitive process.

Consider that there are three levels of thought for deep thinking. Level 1 is lower order thinking where an individual simply relies on gut intuition. Level 2 thinking allows an individual to be selective about what they choose to reflect on but is not using critical thinking. Level 3 is an explicit reflection at the highest skill level and routinely uses critical thinking skills.

Intelligence is what you think whereas metacognition is how you think. Regardless of one's intelligence, thinking skills lead them to deeper understanding of how things are related and therefore with understanding a person can exercise wisdom. So, are you a shallow thinker or a deep thinker?

| Shallow Thinkers | Deep Thinkers |
|---|---|
| Cling desperately to their own way of thinking | Are always looking to learn more and think deeper for meaning rather than what they think they know |
| Refuse to better themselves or consider other thinking models, opinions, arguments, principles, frameworks, and patterns that question their perceptions | Put forth effort and patience looking for truth |
| Believe everything they read or hear without applying critical thinking or deep understanding | Don't believe everything they hear or read; instead, they research the truth first then decide what they believe |
| Sometimes fail to understand how their words and actions affect others | Examine the consequences of their behavior |

Deep thinking is how we increase our number of valuable and useful thoughts. Deep thoughts allow us to do the things that thinking, planning, research, and applied judgment reveal to us. Anyone can become a deep thinker, but one must realize that it is hard and exhausting. Most people are content with just an easy non-disciplined flow of thoughts. We can choose to be a shallow thinker or a deep thinker. We can apply wisdom with understanding, or we can be a thought drifter. King Solomon became wise by applying himself to the understanding of wisdom and recognizing that shallow thinking and folly are "chasing after the wind."[1] Power Thinkers are deep thinkers who change their lives for the better.

## Disciplined Thought Habits

Discipline leads to habits since habits are established with synaptic nerve pathways in the brain because of repetition. It is a learned experience that takes conscious thought to begin and maintain, which later does not require conscious effort to perform due to memory. Thoughts require energy, and mental energy use can lead to physical fatigue. Recouping that energy with sleep and rest restores the capacity of a person to continue to perform. That is why a correctly formed habit uses less mental energy since it becomes automatic without the requirement of disciplined thought. Good habits assist in more energy for a person to perform at their best.

Discipline is the ability to act in accordance with a chosen system of thought or belief. It is the ability to overcome the inertia of existing actions and act in a new direction. Discipline is strongly associated with willpower. Willpower governs and directs the mind and mind thinks according to the will and governs and directs the body. Discipline tends to be associated with doing things that go against our natural selves. Volition is the voluntary willing power in action.

Habits are the actions that we take without much thought or intention. They are our body's programmed auto-responses to stimuli and situations. They are often overlooked and not thought about precisely because they are automatic, and our conscious mind therefore does not detect them.

Attitudes are habits of thought. On an airplane control panel there are gauges to indicate attitude to keep the wings level and the altitude to determine if the plane is ascending or descending. The pilot, in this case you, is in control of the attitude and altitude. Therefore, it is your habits or thoughts or attitudes that determine your altitudes of accomplishment. Thoughts can lead to powerful outcomes.

Discipline involves training and repetition based upon a will for accomplishment. Will is based upon motives. Motives are a reason for doing something or not doing something based upon values and purpose. Motive is what prompts you to form a desire. Desire is what leads to forming an intention.

The primary difference between intention and motive is that intention specifically indicates the mental state of a person at the time of action, i.e., what's going on in one's mind, at the time of the action. Whereas motive implies the motivation, i.e., what drives a person to do or refrain from doing something. Motive is the reason behind intention. While intention means the purpose of doing something, motive determines the reason for an action. Intention is defined as the desire to bring about a certain result or consequence. Purpose is determination. Intention is a pre-planned purpose. A trigger stimulus happens, a thought where reason is employed predetermines a motive for action (motivation) which is carried out with intention which yields a consequence.

Discipline also is a form of self-control, which is based upon a strong will, which is based upon strong feelings and emotions for action. Self-control is based upon determination. Determination is an intense sense of self-devotion and self-commitment to achieve or perform a given task or to avoid taking an action that has been pre-determined to not be in the best interest of a person.

Disciplined thought habits start with deep thought to discover a "why" that will be acted upon with a "how" to produce a "what." Consistent practice of a predetermined motive is how one develops a major definite purpose, which provides focus and direction for action.

---

## Chapter 5 Summary:
## Power Thinking Tools for Power Leadership

THINKING skills are the mental activities you use to process information, make connections, make decisions, and create innovative ideas. You use your thinking skills when you try to make sense of experiences, solve problems, make decisions, ask questions, make plans, or organize information.

Consider the ideas as to why we should think and why people are afraid of thinking. We should direct our thinking and be in control of our thoughts since this is a great gift from the Creator. Certainly, we should think before speaking or acting. Giving thought to our ways enables us to predict an outcome and continue or reverse course. We will always be glad we thought first and then spoke or acted in a particular way. Thinking can restore common sense, and while we may examine the thoughts of experts, we should not blindly subject ourselves to their thoughts. If the information is an item of interest to us, we can use the thinking skills we learned and become a thought leader on the subject to develop our own expertise in that subject.

Having a skill in thinking is what causes us to first become Leading Thinkers, then with additional skill development, we can become Master Thinkers, and then additional skills allow us to make good decisions, organize our thoughts, and our actions by becoming Power Thinkers. These skills will serve us for a lifetime. The Certified Thought Leader coursework to become a CTL is available at the Center for Quality Leadership and the designations of Leading Thinker, Master Thinker, and Power Thinker are contingent upon completion of the courses as you move through the program. CQL.net is the website.

Skillful thinking can help identify tipping points that lead to change. The reason people may be afraid to think is because they may be afraid of change. Others are not afraid to think because they indeed want change.

Just because you have thoughts doesn't mean you know how to think. We live in an age where numerous people want to place their thoughts in your mind to influence you to their way of thinking. There are several reasons why people allow social influences to affect their thoughts and behavior. One reason is that we often conform to the norms of a group to gain acceptance of its members. But what if it is the wrong group?

Thinking is some of the hardest work, and this may be a reason so few people think skillfully or even bother to think at all. The thinking skills discussed in this chapter are used by some of the most influential and accomplished individuals who have ever lived. Be a Power Thinker and unlock your brain to discover the unknown.

# 6

---

## FINDING YOUR POWER PURPOSE

*People who lack the clarity, courage, or determination to fulfill a dream will always surrender to fear and wonder what happened.*

— GERMANY KENT, ACTRESS, AUTHOR, AND
BROADCAST JOURNALIST

P urpose is your role in life. One can discover and determine a purpose based upon values and strongly held beliefs. This involves a carefully considered mindset.

Develop a strong vision of what needs to be done. To know what a person or a group wants, you must first know what their purpose is for doing something. This begins with the deeply held values, mores, history, experience, stories, and legends about key people and events that have affected an individual or an organization. Letting your mind wander as you wonder about various things will allow your mind and imagination to open and roam all the possibilities, dreams, and ideas that can emerge.

Sometimes a mastermind group lets multiple minds produce ideas that no individual would come up with on their own. A mastermind alliance is the coordination of knowledge and effort, in a spirit of harmony, between two or more people, for the attainment of a definite purpose. Two or more minds come together by creating a third, invisible, intangible force that may be likened to a third mind. The synergy of more than one mind always creates more than either of them alone can create.

Discovering purpose is the process that involves an examination of past practices, reflecting upon the good, the bad, and the ugly of those practices. Considering what went well and what should not be repeated is valuable insight into clarification of what you want and why as you seek to clarify and define your purpose for your life, your career, your organizational purpose, and how you want to spend your nonrefundable fragments of eternity known as time.

This will encounter fear, frustration, and judgment. However, frustration can be replaced with courage, fear can be replaced with excitement, and judgment can be replaced with curiosity. Curiosity will drive new visions that, combined with your existing culture to develop and review your conscience, can lead to the discovery of the passion of your purpose. This will unlock your brain and allow you to imagine doing things that have never been thought of or done before.

Purpose, which is long-term intent and guiding principles, should not be confused with specific goals or business strategies. Strategies are things that often change as goals are reached. Whereas you might achieve a goal or complete a strategy, you cannot fulfill a purpose. A purpose is like a guiding star on the horizon—forever pursued but never quite reached. You can only live a purpose for the duration of your life or the life of your organization. Although purpose itself does not change, it does inspire change, growth, and continued improvement for transformation. Purpose stimulates change and progress. Personal or organizational purpose should create a single unifying principle that connects with one's emotional aspirations and yields a fulfillment of time and energy spent. A purpose is what drives extra effort, creativity, teamwork, and extraordinary focus.

A purpose is connected to long-term deeply held values and beliefs, including the differentiated needs it addresses. We should act on purpose with intentional commitment. A purpose statement describes the overarching reason that gives meaning to an individual or company. Purpose statements are used to help develop a clear value-enhanced vision and then to motivate actions to accomplish the mission and reach goals.

I believe that an individual or company or organization should have a purpose statement, a vision statement, a mission statement, and goals. So, just what does this mean? Should this be a rigid framework? In the past, a common thought was that a mission statement and goals were sufficient to employ strategies and tactics to accomplish what was wanted. So, just which is the most effective approach?

Purpose is when the values encourage certain behaviors that lead to accomplishment. Purpose yields fulfillment of what one is doing with their life or their work, whether it be as an individual or as an organization for a reason. Vision is the clear picture of what is desired and helps provide clarity. Vision keeps you on course to fulfill your purpose. Remember, when clarity is present, decisions are easy. Therefore, it is important to have a very clear vision of the journey you wish to take based upon your clearly identified purpose.

Having a clear picture or vision of what you want and aligning that with the purpose of fulfillment will lead to a mission which is the roadmap and vehicle to take the journey. Next goals are established that are on the way of the journey. Strategies are defined once goals are clarified. Strategies are choices one makes to approach a behavior that will lead to goal accomplishment. The goal may employ different strategies for accomplishment. Since a particular strategy may be replaced with another when persistent attempts to still reach a goal are stifled when roadblocks occur. Tactics are the steps taken incrementally within a strategy to reach the goal which accomplishes a mission in keeping with the vision and yields fulfillment to the purpose.

## Purpose Statement

Purpose is the reason for which something is done or created or for which something exists. Purpose can be used to determine the reason behind a person's doing something, while an objective refers to something a person wants to accomplish. Purpose and objective are often used to refer to something that a person wishes to fulfill or something that he or she intends to achieve or accomplish.

Since purpose serves passion (strong and barely controllable emotion), passion shapes purpose When the idea for a venture or a cause starts taking shape, purpose is what ultimately helps define it and also helps develop the obsession (an idea or thought that continually preoccupies or intrudes on a person's mind) of thought that drives compulsive fixation, preoccupation, and enthusiasm of the mind to develop a vision of where the purpose will take you and by what means the mission will take you on the journey of the vision.

To find your purpose for something, identify the things you care about by making a list of them, prioritizing them, and affirming them or casting them aside. To do this, reflect on what matters most. For example, your legacy. Remember, you can do anything but not everything; therefore, identify what one thing matters the most. Be sure to recognize your strengths and talents. A talent is what comes easy and is fun and fulfilling. Try to imagine various possibilities by using creative thinking. Then, cultivate the emotions that support your purpose and feeds your passion. This will help you develop a proper mindset and motivation to act. This is done when you examine the past and imagine the future by asking who are you, where are you, and why are you here?

This will help you determine what you are willing to spend time on to accomplish what makes you feel fulfilled. Realize that you get one life with fleeting time and energy, so you must determine how you will spend it for optimum fulfillment.

Purpose is the why so ask yourself, "Why the why?" The following sentence may appear to be awkward, it also helps to determine your purpose since purpose is based on reasoned thought that yields a reason for action. So, ask yourself the question, "What is the reason for the reason that has been reasoned with thoughtful thinking? What dominates your thoughts or feelings with a persistent idea, image, or desire?"

Finding your "why" before communicating your "what" or your "how" to the world is critical to both business success and your personal growth. If you don't know your purpose, you cannot clearly communicate or effectively execute your mission.

You cannot stay laser-focused on what you want to build long-term. It'll be easy to veer from your path with many distractions and hard to maintain your inspiration for action.

Power Thinkers have an opportunity to establish consistency of action first, which promotes resilience in the face of social or environmental shocks, and then a differentiated social value proposition. To identify a purpose, a person must identify the why behind the what.

Here are a series of questions to guide a person as they consider a why behind a what. What makes you come alive? What inspires you to want to breathe life into something? What are your innate strengths? What natural talent and skill come together to stir your passion? Where do you add the greatest value? What problems do you enjoy solving with passion? How will you measure your life? What legacy do you want to leave? Legacy is answered by the questions, "Did you get what you wanted, and was it worth it?"

In summary, as Stephen Covey said in his book *7 Habits of Highly Effective People*, "Begin with the end in mind."[1] Consider that this end must be fulfilling of your purpose. Also when you examine your vision or end picture, look for clarity of the reason you have developed a decisive major purpose. This produces a detailed thought which can be combined with specific action, to accomplish anything a person conceives and believes that they can achieve. This is not meant to be a rigid framework, rather it is meant to illuminate the nature and relationship of each of these components as they exist and how they can be employed by Power Thinking.

When you are powered by a clear purpose, there is little you cannot do. If you know and understand what you really want to do and what you really want to be, you will do what matters the most to you and that is what really gives you a sense of purpose. Finding the intersection of these questions gives you the greatest sense of meaning and reward in your life. Purpose is what you are passionate about and helps you to develop a clear determined direction with resolve to accomplish what you focus on.

## Vision, Values, Direction

Once a person or organization has determined their purpose, the next step is to consider the direction that their actions will take them. This should also inspire them to action. The vision provides clarity. In the book *Alice's Adventures in Wonderland*, Alice asks the Cheshire Cat which path she should take. The cat asked her where she wanted to go, and she said she didn't know. The cat then replied that any path would do. Alice lacked a sense of purpose and direction. We can become Alice on any given day. Therefore, we need to examine purpose and then think about what direction we should take to fulfill our passion determined by our purpose.

The vision based upon purpose leads our thoughts to the journey we wish to take to fulfill our purpose. This will be inspiring and helps to develop in our mind's eye the possibilities that are available to us as we dream about our future. It helps to clarify our aim and direction. It engages the happy chemicals in our brain and gives us the energy to then establish our mission. This will focus our thoughts, energy, actions, behavior, and decisions toward things that matter most and will help to avoid getting distracted. It says what you want your life to be and who you want to become as a person or organization.

Now that we have discovered our purpose and our vision, our mission is the vehicle or means that we will employ to serve the purpose while taking the journey to fulfill our purpose. The mission is like a roadmap. It is only at this point that goals are established and strategies and tactics are considered. Without the why behind the where, what good is the how and the what? In other words, the why is the purpose, the where is the vision or where we want to go, the how is the mission, and the what are the goals, strategies, and tactics that are employed to fulfill the purpose. The development of these using Power Thinking is what mindful thought leaders do. Here is an example of purpose, vision, and mission statements for the Center for Quality Leadership (CQL):

**CQL Purpose**
Provide wisdom for using our mind to discover the unknown possibilities to design our future.

**CQL Vision**
Provide clarity of thought that enables individuals to recognize, review, and analyze any situation or problem and use a mindful approach with thinking skills to imagine and create a solution that improves, advances, or even changes the direction of important decisions.

**CQL Mission**
Equipping individuals to think, by utilizing quality systems, tools, and processes for productive learning and living.

Now it is easier to use our minds to discover the unknown. Now goals will have meaning and purpose as well as motivation to reach them. Now it is easier to develop a mindset and a major definite purpose. Now it is easier to organize our thoughts for organized and focused action. With clarity, decisions are easier. Daily review of these plans will compound the performance for accomplishment because that behavior creates new neural pathways in our brains and forms new habits.

## Plans

Planning bridges the gap between where we are and where we want to go. Planning equips the mission to go on the journey of the vision to accomplish the purpose. Planning encourages innovative ideas, aids decision-making, and requires thinking in advance about what to do and how to do it. In short, planning is thinking.

Plans are detailed roadmaps for execution of actions identified to reach goals that are established and to recognize possible strategies and tactics to employ to reach the goals. Goals are then broken down into measurable objectives based upon a work breakdown structure or reverse engineering by thinking about what one wants to accomplish and identifying the small steps that must be taken to accomplish an objective that leads to accomplishment of the goals. Plans must be written in detail so daily action can be taken. Until targeted objectives are identified, no effective action can be taken.

As was mentioned earlier, executive stewardship involves leading people and managing things. Plans are things to be managed, but they involve people, which is where leadership comes in. The executive or decision-making part of the brain is part of neuroscience. A common term now is "neuro leadership," which involves understanding that behavior in planning and execution of the plans involves habits of behavior for people to either succeed or fail to accomplish their goals. Habits are a result of brain pathways being established in the brain of each person affected by the plan. This involves collaboration, decision-making, influencing people, organizational behavior, leadership, social interactions, and building trust with others. All the aforementioned items involve thinking and mindfulness of interacting with others and certain mindsets necessary for the execution of plans.

It is not uncommon for a particular leader to mastermind a plan to do something unique, new, or innovative. Power Thinkers who have become mind masters can work in collaboration with other thinkers to produce a particular plan, adventure, or history-changing course of activities that lead others to phenomenal results.

## Performance

Performance involves the creation of systems and processes to execute the plans and accomplish the goals using the vehicle of the mission to take the journey of the vision to fulfill the purpose we have determined based upon our deeply held values and beliefs. Performance involves setting our mindset to align with our purpose, vision, mission, and goals. To do this, we should become a Mind Master so that we can mastermind the plan. A Mind Master is someone who understands how the mind works and who realizes that whatever they conceive and believe they can achieve. A Mind Master takes control of their own thoughts, understands how the brain works, imagines possibilities, dreams big, looks for insight, discerns the consequences of actions, and applies their heart to elite performance. In other words, a Mind Master is a Power Thinker.

They exercise creative vision (discovering opportunities),

define their major purpose (prioritization) and develop and implement an action plan with detail (commitment). A high-performance mindset removes obstacles and mental limitations by implementing a disciplined approach to discovering opportunities, prioritizing them, and using mental tools such as a mind map to capture thoughts, also they exercise an affinity diagram to generate, organize, and consolidate information concerning a product, process, complex issue, or problem. Next, they create an interrelationship diagraph to determine cause and effects of the complex ideas. They utilize deep thinking, first principles thinking, and second order thinking. Second order thinking asks the question, "and then what?" Second order thinking is the process of tracing down and unraveling the implications of those first order impacts. Jeff Boss in his May 15, 2019 article in *Entrepreneur* magazine lists the following famous quote from the elite Navy SEAL (Sea, Air, and Land) teams is. "There are only two ways in which to do something—the right way, and again."[2] They condition their thinking, and, therefore their attitudes and actions for extraordinary performance. If a particular task is worth doing, then it's worth doing correctly. However, if the process is valued as much, if not more, than the outcome, then there will never be a wrong way; there will only be another way. That's the powerful message that the Navy SEAL teams promote.

Humans are emotional creatures. However, we can control our impulses. Navy SEAL training uses that factor to rewire the brains of the SEAL graduates to properly respond to the unpredictable and the unknown by changing how their brains react to extraordinary circumstances. Controlling fear and emotions in an instant is crucial to their battlefield success. While our businesses may not proceed with the chaos of a warzone, it is necessary to train our brains to be observant, mindful, aware. and respond thoughtfully in all that we do through concentration, focus, and maintaining a deep embodied attention to not only a plan but also the performance of leading the execution of that plan.

Mark Divine, a former Navy SEAL Commander and founder of SEAL Fit and the Halo Effect, spoke at a recent conference of mine and taught us about box breathing and meditation exercises so that elite performance behaviors can be developed. Deep breathing can enhance brain activity. Long exhales get more oxygen to the brain and allow us to make better decisions. These techniques are based upon neuroscience of the brain and Power Thinking.

---

## Chapter 6 Summary:
## Finding Your Power Purpose

WE SHOULD ACT on purpose and with purpose once we discover our major definite purpose. Purpose is the why behind what we want to do. If we don't know this why, then it may not make sense to do the what. By knowing the why, we will be able to do it more skillfully. This will give us mental clarity to know what to focus on. Just like a laser, which is a coherent electromagnetic field, we can develop laser-like thoughts. In a coherent beam of electromagnetic energy, all the waves have the same frequency and phase. When our thoughts are aligned to the same frequency and in the same concentrated focus, we can organize our thoughts and our plans to stay concentrated on what we want to accomplish. Lasers are powerful and laser thinking is Power Thinking.

Discovering your purpose will guide you on your journey.

Purpose is what you are passionate about and helps you to develop a clear, determined direction with resolve to accomplish what you focus on. Once the purpose is known, it is easier to engage in the thinking required for effective planning to perform efficiently.

Planning is important for accomplishment. However, it is interesting to take note that the planning may be more important than the plan itself. The thought process involved in planning engages the brain creatively. This process is important, but plans can change due to unforeseen circumstances. When unforeseen circumstances occur and the plan must be revised, the brain exercise involved in the planning makes it easier to reflect, review, adapt, and it will allow you to overcome unforeseen circumstances.

The processes we have discussed influences our behavior to take our performance to a greater level of success. Elite performance by a Power Thinker makes you part of a select group that has developed superb skills that gives you the advantage of superior performance based upon skill, ability, commitment, and accomplishment because of how you think and what you think about to behave as a peak performer.

# POWERFUL PLANNING TOOLS TO ORGANIZE THOUGHT FOR ACCOMPLISHMENT

*The best way to predict the future is to create it.*

— PETER DRUCKER

G oals are only reached with purpose based upon desire plus determination (mindset). This is the why behind the what. Practical wisdom combined with personal initiative to go the extra mile for individual achievement is the basis of all achievement. It deals with the quantity and quality of service. Accomplishment comes from imagination and creativity with practical implementation. Ideas are the beginning of all achievements.

## Characteristics of a Power Thinker

Don't let your thoughts limit you. We draw in what we constantly think about. Our lives follow our thoughts. Think power thoughts. Be confident, think positively. Think on success not on failure. Realize that the forces that are for you are greater than the forces that are against you because of the way you control your thoughts. If you think you can, you can. If you think you can't, you can't. It all starts in our minds and depends upon our thinking. Thoughts have power. Negative thoughts have negative power over a negative thinker. Positive, confident, assertive thoughts have a powerful impact over a power thinker. The battle for defeat or victory is taking place in your mind. You are full of can-do power if you do not harbor limiting and negative fearful thoughts. Power thinkers see the same giant oppositions and risks that negative and fearful thinkers see, but instead of thinking defeated thoughts, they think power thoughts, thoughts that empower them to believe in their success and look for activities to succeed. You would not be facing the obstacles if you couldn't handle them. Be confident in your ability to think through challenges and find solutions. Victory is achieved by those who are dedicated, committed, determined, and alert to opportunities to win regardless of the effort it takes to think it, see it, and do it. Don't look at how big the obstacles are, look at how big Infinite Intelligence is and its power to overcome any obstacle. That obstacle is no match for Infinite Intelligence, which you have access to through belief. All things are possible for Infinite Intelligence.

Keep a cycle of power thoughts for success rather than a negative cycle of fear, defeat, discouragement, and delay of action. The energy of positive or negative thoughts will consume you. It is up to you to select positive power thoughts. How you think is everything. Every morning when Power Thinkers wakeup, they power up by the thoughts that they are in a habit of thinking. They take advantage of rest and strength to set the tone for the day. Morning habits can literally determine the success or failure for that day. Therefore, establish powerful thinking habits to engage each morning regardless of circumstances. Think, *This is going to be a good day. I can manage anything that comes my way. I am strong, I am confident, I have Infinite Intelligence as my guide.* At the start of the day, set your day's mindset for victory. Be purposeful in your thinking rather than spending time thinking about whatever comes to mind or is influenced by the news or social media. You are the master of your destiny, the captain of your soul. Be careful about what you think. Your thoughts set the limit for your life. Get rid of defeated thoughts and think power thoughts. Look at your blessings and gifts with an eye of gratitude and think about how abundant your future will be. Remember the Law of the Harvest—you reap what you sow. Ralph Waldo Emerson is known for the following poem, which was used by Steven Covey in his book *7 Habits of Highly Effective People:*[1]

> *Sow a thought reap an action;*
> *sow an action, reap a habit;*
> *sow a habit, reap a character;*
> *sow a character, reap a destiny.*

The quality of your thoughts determines the quality of your actions and the quality of your life. Be a Power Thinker. Forget the past and press on to the future. This is the key difference between a negative mental attitude and a positive mental attitude and the difference between a fixed mindset and a growth mindset.

Character descends from the heart, competence descends from the mind, consequences descend from the body, and leadership descends from the spirit. It all begins with your thoughts. Thought is the only thing you have complete control over. Therefore, use this power wisely and skillfully.

It takes character and competence to develop the will to act appropriately. Walk in the ways of insight and wisdom. Wisdom will reward you. Wisdom comes to a character that develops competence to select consequences based upon information, knowledge, and understanding.

A discerning character is developed with the habit of being insightful. Use all your senses, the five physical senses and the sixth spiritual sense, to develop insight into wise actions. Develop a growth mindset to always be seeking knowledge and learning to develop understanding to act with wisdom. Develop sound judgment and exercise discernment. Always be seeking wisdom to use the heart to develop the will to apply understanding to your actions.

Recognize and apply opportunities. Set your heart and then set your mind. Look carefully, listen closely, and give attention to wisdom and understanding, taking hold with all your heart. Meditate on the exact thing that is consuming your thoughts as a desirable thing to do, have, or be as a person. Your mind will grow stronger in this exercise. Meditation is a skill and practice that is required to become a Power Thinker. Fill every spare moment with thought about what you truly desire rather than being distracted with email, social media, and other distracting things. Pursue what you want and focus on it with obsessive burning, white-hot desire. Read, think, research, and explore everything related to what you want. Use your capacity to pause and ponder the why, the what, and the how of achieving what you set your mind on. Exercise deep thinking on the truths and realities that you have discovered. This disciplined approach with a humble attitude is what sets you apart from your peers.

What do you really want? Is it a wish or a true accomplishment on which you will definitely act? Is this your definite major purpose? Are you willing to act on purpose with purpose? Where did you get this idea? Why do you think and believe you can and should do it?

This book is about thinking. Asking questions causes a person to think. Asking a series of quality questions is important because the quality of the questions determines the quality of the answer for appropriate action. Having a clear vision for what it is you want to accomplish comes only from deep thought that starts with the imagination and creative thinking portion of the brain and then engaging the linear portion of the brain in concert to clearly identify the exact thing you wish to accomplish. Some people think that they are either identified as a left brain or linear thinker or a right brain creative artist. The truth of the matter is that we have been given the ability to do both by our Creator. We can be whole brain thinkers as I have explained in the section on executive stewardship. We can and should engage all parts of our brain.

## Fact, Faith, Feeling

Faith and belief that something is possible combined with a strong feeling or emotion to act combined with action is why is it said that whatever the mind of a person can conceive and believe, it can achieve. Napoleon Hill and W. Clement Stone worked together to promote this philosophy. Paul J. Meyer states it a little differently. He says, "Whatever you vividly imagine, ardently desire, sincerely believe, and enthusiastically act upon, must inevitably come to pass."[2] I have personally met both W. Clement Stone and Paul J. Meyer. A plaque with Paul's quote hangs in my office and an autographed copy of the book by W. Clement Stone sits on my bookshelf. The principles mentioned in these quotes are the same and have been proven numerous times by many individuals.

Guarding your thoughts and your heart are extremely important to successful thinking and action. The reason is that while confidence exists, the counterpart known as fear also exists. Fear is the mind killer.

Power Thinkers exercise systematic thinking combined with methodical action. They develop a process for accomplishments. They understand that their behavior and actions lead to outcomes. They know that having clear goals leads to clear results. Their success starts with a decision to read, think, ask questions, and then make disciplined decisions. Next, they resolve to accomplish and engage the power of will, to make the accomplishment. Each act they perform is with fidelity, righteousness, and uprightness of heart on the right path.

Are you a wantrepreneur or an entrepreneur? Don't just love the idea, act on it. Kevin O'Leary, a billionaire on the TV show *Shark Tank*, says in his book *Cold Hard Truth: On Business, Money & Life* to find a problem everyone has and solve it.[3] He advises to use hustle and savvy combined with a driving innovative force. If you want to make a lot of money, don't learn from someone who has no money. Learn from those who have had the vision, taken the action with persistence, and accomplished what they set out to do. People like that are people like you. You too can discover the unknown by engaging in Power Thinking. Don't be afraid to tackle the largest issues. Engage in problem identification and description, use creative thinking and innovation.

How do you find a problem everyone has and solve it, or how do you turn a goal into a problem? First, write a problem statement that identifies and explains the problem in a concise but detailed way to give a comprehensive view of what's going on. Identifying who the problem impacts, what the impacts are, where the problem occurs, and why and when it needs to be fixed. Without the problem statement, the problem may not be obvious to anyone. Frame the problem in a way that helps illuminate viable solutions. This will clarify what the expected outcomes are. Then examine a variety of solutions and propose a carefully selected solution and scope of the solution to make clear what you propose to happen. Make sure that your analysis is accurate and that you are identifying the right problem to solve without creating another problem. Misdiagnosis of what is going on can mean that you start treating the wrong problem. Accurate thinking is important. Problem-solving involves thought and understanding. Problems can be represented by chain diagrams, tree diagrams, flow charts, or simple lists. It is often useful to try multiple representations to discover a proper fit.

Next, identify and explain the root cause of the problem. Use creative thinking with analysis and synthesis to propose a best solution to the problem. Demonstrate through implementation of the solution that this is the best outcome.

What is the discrepancy between what is expected and what is occurring?

Problem Identification

Problem Analysis

Why is the problem occurring? Identify the root cause.

**Problem Solving**

Is the proposed solution effective?

Plan Evaluation

Plan Development

What is the detailed proposed solution?

Plan Implementation

How will implementation integrity and fidelity be ensured?

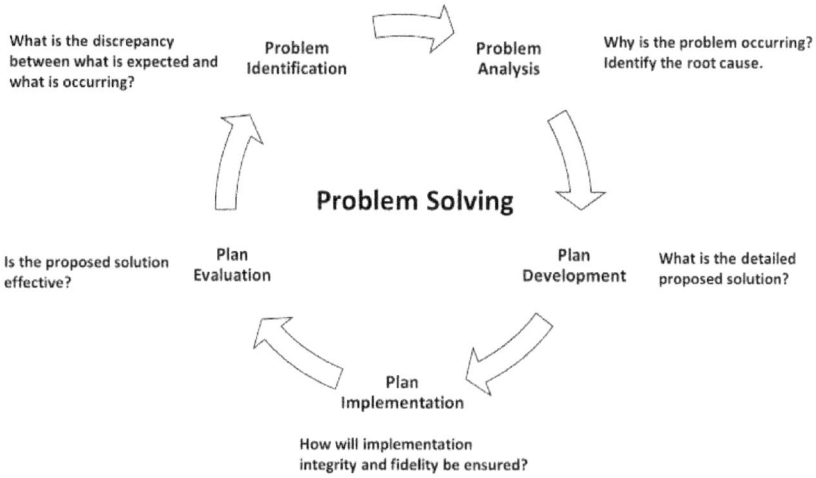

There are a number of root cause tools. A simple one to use is the five whys tool because it helps you determine root cause quickly. If you have examined a young child asking questions, you no doubt have observed the five whys method without realizing it. Frequently, a child will ask a question and then get an answer that they ponder and then ask why? This process is repeated naturally until a level of understanding is reached that satisfies the questioner. The following is a sample of that process.

## The Five Whys Root Cause Analysis Model

| Define the Problem Insert one of the top prioritized items in the problem identification | | | | | |
|---|---|---|---|---|---|
| Step 1 | Why is it happening? | Answer 1 | | | |
| | Step 2 | Why is that? | Answer 2 | | |
| | | Step 3 | Why is that? | | |
| | | | Step 4 | Answer 3 | |
| | | | | Step 5 | Answer 4 |
| | | | | | Why is that? |
| Note: Record solution ideas that fit each level | | | | | |

As you push for deeper whys, record all your ideas. You can then arrange them with other thinking tools for further analysis and synthesis. A fishbone diagram is another example of a cause and effect as you search for the root cause. It is like the five whys in that it takes each issue and asks the why questions.

**Bones are the Major Cause Categories**

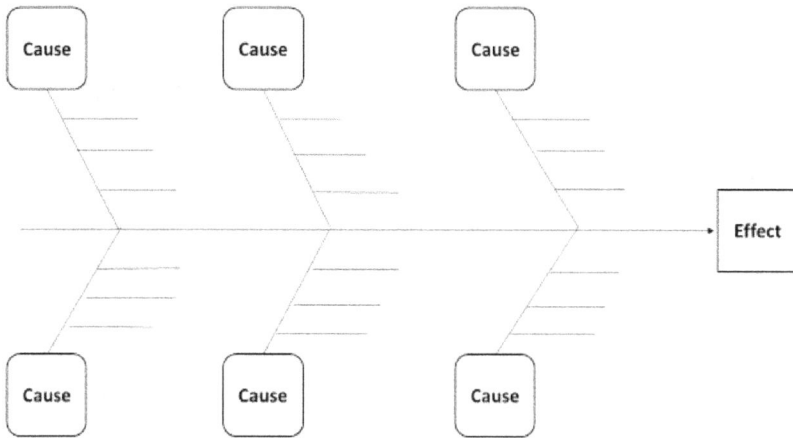

Keep in mind that impossible is an opinion. Know your purpose, practice, and performance and don't panic when challenged. There is a fine line between prudence and panic. When you feel like panic, remember to pause, breathe, engage your mental capabilities, and select a prudent action; this helps avoid panic. Keep your wits about you.

Michael Easter, in his February 8, 2021, article published in *Medium* says that when he was writing his book *The Comfort Crises* he interviewed Trevor Kashey regarding goal setting and Trevor told him, "Goals feel good to set, but they're just a diversion. People face no consequence if they don't reach their goal. So they forget it and set another one again and mess that one up, too." [4]

Solving a problem is inherently more tactical and specific than working toward a goal. Solving a problem involves both strategic and tactical efforts which lead to goal accomplishment.

Power Thinkers are problem solvers who use a combination of intuition and logical reasoning to come up with solutions while employing thinking skills to discover all aspects of a problem, while keeping in mind the difference in complex and simple thinking. They clearly define the problem and examine hidden opportunities that may be revealed while thinking deeply about the problem. They then explore options and combinations of options to find the right solution. Permutations of these options depend upon a rearrangement of the elements of opportunities in a certain order of things. Combinations do not rely on any given order and do not also require taking all of them as a set. It is okay to select a partial set or even the complete set.

Most people are challenged when it comes to establishing order and becoming organized. Napoleon Hill mentions in his book *Think and Grow Rich* the concept of organized thought and organized action.[5] What are the benefits of organization? One of the benefits is control. When you have control of your thoughts, it allows you to find things faster, make contact quicker, and get things done. These are critical to accomplish what you want and later follow up on the things that you have an idea to do. Interruptions are frequent and ubiquitous, but an organized action plan based upon organized thoughts keeps interruptions from becoming disruptions.

Without order, chaos creeps in. Chaos is not your friend. Chaos is the evil force that creates despair and doubt and drains energy from your thoughts and your deeds. Chaos is the opposite of order. Chaos causes drifting, which leads to the road to nowhere. This a prime example of chaos and the lack of organized thinking, which of course must precede organized action. One of the most important tasks is to determine exactly what purpose one wants to accomplish and why. The why should always precede the what and how and when and why then. Next, the brain must be engaged to creatively determine a pathway.

Remember that there is power in synergy. Synergy is when the interaction or coordination of two or more people or substances or organizations interact to combine for an effect greater than the sum of their separate effects. This is true of people, books or other stimuli combined with concentrated thought to produce organization for accomplishment. Frequently this is referred to as a mastermind. Mastermind summits and conferences are designed to capture the synergy of thinkers and to engage with thought leaders to seek new ideas or to further build upon existing thought experiments.

Courage comes from the heart, which is the seat of the emotions. Napoleon Hill, in his book *How to Own Your Own Mind,* indicates that there are nine basic motives that initiate desire, which leads to willpower through volition.[6] The nine basic motives are: emotion of love, emotion of sex, desire for health, desire for self-expression, desire for freedom of body and mind, desire for personal expression and fame, desire for perpetuation of life, desire for revenge, and the emotion of fear. Fear is based upon fear of poverty, fear of criticism, fear of ill health, fear of loss of love, fear of old age, fear of loss of liberty, and fear of death.

Power Thinkers develop a strong vision of what needs to be done, take a definite stance on why it needs to be done and with the clarity as to why they are the one to do it is how they develop a major definite purpose. Power Thinkers also do a focus heat map, reviewing consequences of doing it or not doing it.

In the following figure, the consequences scale ranges from not important to critically important with significant consequences. This also parallels from not being a priority to a top priority. The urgency scale ranges from accomplishment "sometime" to the highest scale of "critical and immediate." As an action moves up the consequence scale and to the critical urgency scale, it moves into the red zone of the heat map. Since passion creates fuel for action this heat map assists a Power Thinker in choosing appropriate action at any given point.

**Priority Heat Map**

| | | | | | | | |
|---|---|---|---|---|---|---|---|
| Impact of Importance (Consequences) | Priority A1 | Critically Important with significant consequences | | | | | Top Priority |
| | Priority A | Very Important consequences | | | | | |
| | Priority B | Important consequences | | | | | |
| | Priority C | Moderately Important consequences | | | | | |
| | Priority D | Not Important | | | | | |
| | | | Insignificant (Sometime) | Minor (This Month) | Moderate (This Week) | Urgent (Today) | Critical (Immediately) |

**Scale of Current Urgency (How Much It Matters Right Now)**
**Passion: intensity of desire to accomplish something**
**Passion creates fuel for action**

Thinking precedes action but may lead to right or wrong action. What are the risks of wrong priorities? Do you still have the courage to act?

## OODA Loop (Observe, Orient, Decide, Act)

The OODA Loop is a cycle of thinking where one observes their situation, orients themselves to the best advantage, decides what to do next, and acts on that decision.

This is now used by the Navy SEAL teams and other combat ready forces at the operational level during military campaigns. It is now also often applied to understand nonmilitary operations and learning processes. It assists in assessing quickly what is the next priority for action. This also leads to process improvement. In Total Quality Management practices, the cycle similar to OODA is the Shewhart Cycle or as W. Edwards Deming applied it as the Plan Do Check Act (PDCA) cycle. Others apply it as the Plan Do Study Act (PDSA) cycle. These are a couple of the management and planning tools that are widely used in business. The Shewhart cycle or Shewhart learning and improvement cycle combine management thinking with statistical analysis. The constant evaluation of management policy and procedures leads to continuous improvement. Shewhart was a statistician, and Deming is credited with leading the quality revolution in Japan in the 1950s and later in the 1980s in American business practices for continuous improvement.

In a crisis, whether it is a dangerous crisis such as battlefield experiences or the pressure and crisis of business, Power Thinkers use a technique that combines the physical with the mental. Our brain is our most important organ and is optimized with a proper amount of oxygen. That is why we should pause, breathe, and think before acting. The practice of resilience response stops the brain stem's fear-based reaction to allow the frontal cortex to engage your memories which is where your moral values experience is stored and allows reasonings to engage before action. Breathing restores oxygen to that portion of the brain that allows you to think clearly with the cerebral cortex of the brain so that the reactionary portion of the brain doesn't take choices away. Breathe deeply to regain control. The OODA practice then allows us to think, observe to see what and who is impacted by what is happening, and evaluate impacts as we plan. We then orient to the new reality to see what we have learned so that appropriate action can be taken. Persistence allows emotional control. Emotions must be properly channeled. Emotional awareness and control can be achieved. Another way of thinking about it is that mindfulness is pausing breathing and observing thoughts and emotions so that we can transform energy by transmutation of emotions.

This enables us to learn fast and to choose wisely what we need to know. This has an array of choice since you can learn anything but not everything. Therefore, choose what not to learn so that you can focus on what you should and need to learn. Complex situations can be transformed into "simplexity," which must become simplicity with clarity to secure focus in complex situations. Focus allows us to be clear about our why. Certainty is incremental. We must look for authentic data to create information leading to knowledge, understanding, and wisdom.

In the quality movement mentioned earlier where Deming worked with Japan to bring it out of the devastation of World War II and into respected business excellence, the term *"kaizen"* was recognized as a continuous improvement cycle that leads to breakthrough performance. *Kaizen* is a Japanese term for improvement, and we have adapted it to mean continuous improvement in our business practices. This is how we develop competence.

There are several levels of competence. Of course, the opposite of competence is incompetence. We may not be conscious of our competence or our incompetence. Competence is our ability to do something successfully and efficiently. We can move from unconscious incompetence to conscious incompetence, then to conscious competence, and finally to unconscious competence. What that means is that at the unconscious incompetence level, we have the wrong intuition about something. In fact, we are ignorant of it. Once we discover that we don't know what we may want to know, we can move to the level of conscious incompetence where we realize that we have a wrong analysis of something. Then we move to conscious competence where we have learned the proper analysis of something. Next, we move to unconscious competence where we have the right intuition about something because of our journey from unconscious incompetence to the automatic stage of unconscious competence.

It is important for us to recognize the foregoing journey from not knowing what we do not know to knowing that we know something and can apply that knowledge at will. This allows us to begin challenging the unknown (fear) with action. We can uncover the blind spots in our own thinking. Ignorance is not bliss for Power Thinkers and thought leaders.

If you ever wondered how someone can go from knowing nothing about a topic to becoming the resident expert, you can bet that their secret is weaponized obsession. This is what Power Thinkers and thought leaders do. While there may be a point at which obsession becomes unhealthy, it is possible to use obsession as a tool and be purposeful with it. Obsession is clarity. Healthy obsession is necessary to develop our will to succeed. Obsession is the domination of one's thoughts or feelings by a persistent idea, image, desire, etc.

Obsession is something that burns in your mind persistently. That image, desire, and idea is going to sit there, ever-present in your mind while you go about your day and your work. It will give you the urge to seek out more and more information. It will give you the courage to reach out to others who have gone before you. It will spark inspiration where you thought you could not be inspired. Throw yourself obsessively into your work, imagine what you will be able to accomplish if you throw caution to the wind and allow yourself to become obsessed with your passions.

When you learn to obsess in your passion, you will be suddenly getting a clear vision for what it is you want. By actively participating in your passion, you'll begin seeing it even more clearly. You'll learn what you want to learn, you'll see avenues and opportunities where you would never have seen them and begin creating a network of options for yourself. Clarity begets action, and action begets opportunity. This also engages our creative imagination. Keen imagination is developed through use. We must not neglect this important fact. Remember, motive plus action plus willpower equals persistence. Persistence plus controlled attention equals focus. And focus engages a strong will for accomplishment. When we share this with a carefully chosen close associate in a mastermind alliance, we can achieve greatness because the alliance of two or more in perfect harmony with a definite purpose creates genius.

## Imagination, Creativity, Ideas Matter

Dr. Elmer Gates, a renowned scientist, always looked for new ideas to develop and accomplish. In his book *The Relations and Development of the Mind and Brain,* he talks about the source of his ideas.

1. Knowledge stored in the subconscious mind and acquired through individual experience, observation, and education.
2. Knowledge accumulated by others through the same media, which may be communicated by telepathy.
3. The great universal storehouse of Infinite Intelligence

wherein is stored all knowledge and all facts, and which may be contacted through the subconscious section of the mind.

Gates took the time to concentrate and think in his search for something more. Much like second level thinking by asking "and then what?" as he focused on exactly what he was looking for. He then followed through with positive action. This is consistent with what we are learning in neuroscience. We can and should remodel our thinking from time to time.

## Creative Vision Plus Motive

We are created in the image of the Creator. Hence, we are given the capacity to also be creative. We were also given free will to do or not do anything of our choosing. This is a wonderful gift that should be engaged for good. But first, let's examine what will stifle our creativity so that we can avoid it. If autonomy and freedom are critical to unlocking our creativity, then we should avoid anything that stifles either our autonomy or our freedom to think our own thoughts, let our imaginations be free and express ourselves as we are led to. Excessive restraint is the number one cause of stifled creativity. Meaningless work and activities that consume our time and energy are also creativity killers. Fear and risk aversion likewise are creativity killers. Remembering past failures or seeing others fail along with the fear of failure can cause a person to seek comfort in the known rather than to explore the unknown. Staying busy all the time in a routine that produces little and not taking time to retreat, reflect, and renew will also stifle creativity. When you allow someone else to do the thinking and you're merely responding to what they say, you are not in control of your thoughts.

A freedom-based government like what the United States was founded upon is critical to be creative. Once while I was traveling in a communist-controlled country, I asked the driver of the vehicle I was riding in what his goals were. He told me, "You don't understand. In a communist country, a person does not have the luxury of setting goals." Communism stifles personal creativity. Without trying to be political, the education system in any country must encourage individuals to think, learn, and grow. Holocaust survivor Viktor Frankl, an Austrian neurologist, psychiatrist, philosopher, and author of *Man's Search for Meaning* overcame the fear and restriction to stifle creativity. He got his doctor of medicine degree where he specialized in neurology and psychiatry, with a focus on depression and suicide prior to his internment in a concentration camp. Later he earned his doctor of philosophy degree. He witnessed many who gave up on life due to the very harsh conditions in concentration camps. He also observed that those who had a purpose were able to persevere, overcome, and survive. He used creative vision to create a psychotherapeutic approach, which involved identifying a purpose in life to feel positive about, and then using an immersive imagination of that purpose and its outcome.

Another example of always thinking positively is revealed in the novel *Pollyanna* by Eleanor H. Porter.[7] A young girl named Pollyanna comes to an embittered town and confronts its attitude with her determination to see the best in life. Pollyanna always found something to be grateful for. Today the term "Pollyanna" means a person characterized by irrepressible optimism and a tendency to find good in everything. We are indeed able to find meaning and purpose and use our creativity to stay mentally optimistic and positive if we choose to do so. Don't let creativity killers stifle you.

Creative vision is the ability to recognize opportunities and take action to benefit from them. Certainly, imagination is a critical element of creative vision. Being creative involves consistently producing a lot of ideas. It also involves putting existing ideas together in different combinations. Additionally, it involves breaking an idea down to take a fresh look at its parts. One can also make connections between the topic at hand and seemingly unrelated facts, events, or observations. We are naturally creative and should engage in creative thinking regularly. We must guard against the aforementioned creativity killers and feed our creative spirit. Authentic and original creativity is possible by thinking and discovering something that has never been thought of before by anyone. The most common creativity is found in innovation. Innovation requires a high degree of creativity. Creativity is the process of generating many ideas while innovation is the process of selecting, combining, refining, and turning the best creative ideas into reality. These two are symbiotically connected. When we give our subconscious mind an assignment to mull over with deep thought, we will be amazed at its ability to connect with Infinite Intelligence and link to memories stored in our brain of stimulants that we may not have consciously registered or remembered to produce a creative idea.

A popular and useful technique in creative thinking is the use of mind maps while brainstorming. Brainstorming was introduced as an activity when Alex Osborne wrote the book *Applied Imagination*. Basically, the concept is to attack a problem from numerous directions with the combined force of a group of minds. This is an activity that can be done with or without a mastermind group but is most effective when the participants are truly focused on and committed to the problem at hand. Remember the synergy of connected brains discovering thoughts that none of the individual thinkers would have thought of on their own. There are several tools and techniques to capture thoughts, but a very useful one is a mind map.

A mind map is an easy way to brainstorm thoughts organically without worrying about order and structure. It allows you to visually structure your ideas to help with analysis and recall. A mind map is a diagram for representing tasks, words, concepts, or items linked to and arranged around a central concept or subject using a nonlinear graphical layout that allows the user to build an intuitive framework around a central concept. A mind map can turn a long list of monotonous information into a colorful, memorable, and highly organized diagram that works in line with your brain's natural way of doing things. A mind map is a highly effective way of getting information in and out of your brain—it is a creative and logical means of note taking and note-making that literally "maps out" your ideas. There are many software tools to assist in this process. My favorite so far is an app on my iPad called SimpleMind+. A Power Thinker is always thinking about different topics, and this app allows me to capture individual thoughts about anything and move on to other mind maps for other thoughts that I am exploring. During brainstorming or thinking time, it is important to capture ideas that can be fleshed out in greater detail at another time or to delve deeply into at the time they come into my mind.

After we have an idea, what becomes a reason for action? This becomes our motive? Does it fit one of the nine basic motives based upon emotions that we have previously discussed, or is there a different motive? What do we desire and why? The more reasons you have for doing something, the higher your motivation becomes. That is why we must spend time examining the reasons we would do or not do something. If we cannot identify sufficient reasons to do something, then it shouldn't be done. This involves decision-making.

A useful tool to assist in this is the T-chart developed by Benjamin Franklin. Franklin had a methodical mindset. He also was focused on self-improvement and character development. This tool weighs the pros and cons of doing anything. How is this useful in determining motive? It is useful because it clarifies the reasons to do or not do something. His method was to take a piece of paper and divide it down the middle. On the one side list all the reasons something should or could be done. On the other side, list all the reasons something should not or could not be done. Examine the reasons and weigh the importance of each and then decide if there is sufficient reason (motive) for action. The next most important thing to do is to act. Motivation doesn't cause action, rather action creates motivation. Action releases brain chemicals and creates neural pathways in our brains, which form habits and increase action based upon clear reason for the action, which is our motive.

## Planning and Organized Thought

Planning is a thought process directed toward accomplishment of a definite purpose. Accomplishment takes time. So just what is time, and how does this relate to planning? Eternity is the ever-present with no beginning and no end. Time has a beginning, a measurement of progress, and an end. We sometimes emphasize a period of time. A competitive game usually has a time limit set for the game for things to be done or plays to be run. Thinkers have given certain wisdom regarding time for our consideration.

For example, the Pareto principle, developed by Vilfredo Pareto also known as the 80/20 rule is useful. 80 percent of the benefits are derived from 20 percent of the activities, while 20 percent of the benefits come from 80 percent of the activities. If there was a way to know the 20 percent that give an 80 percent payoff, then we could eliminate most activities that yield little or no benefit. That is what I call warp time. We then are operating at warp speed.

Another proven benefit is to understand Parkinson's law. Cyril Northcote Parkinson, a British naval historian and author, first presented the idea that work expands to fill the available amount of time allotted to it.[8] That means that if you set aside an hour to do a task, it will take the whole hour even if it is discovered that the task could be done in much less time. It is not always easy to estimate how much time a task will take. Prior experience and learning to be more efficient will assist in setting deadlines that are realistic and time-efficient. It is possible to collapse time by thinking clearly and acting quickly with deliberate intent. Time, energy, and expertise go hand in hand to make efficient and effective use of activity to produce excellence.

**Time Pictures**

A time picture is not a photograph, but it is a tool to examine targets for excellent use of time. I suggest a weekly, monthly, and annual time picture for optimum performance. The following is a blank form to create a weekly time picture. This is a guide to determine what routines and areas of focus you intend to give on any given day and the amount of time you intend to devote to it. Keep in mind the 80/20 rule of high-payoff activities and the

Pareto principle for expansion and compression of effort and activity.

## Weekly Time Picture

| Name | | | | Date: | | | |
|---|---|---|---|---|---|---|---|
| | Monday | Tuesday | Wednesday | Thursday | Friday | Saturday | Sunday |
| 5 am | | | | | | | |
| 6 am | | | | | | | |
| 7 am | | | | | | | |
| 8am | | | | | | | |
| 9 am | | | | | | | |
| 10 am | | | | | | | |
| 11 am | | | | | | | |
| Noon | | | | | | | |
| 1 pm | | | | | | | |
| 2 pm | | | | | | | |
| 3 pm | | | | | | | |
| 4 pm | | | | | | | |
| 5 pm | | | | | | | |
| 6 pm | | | | | | | |
| 7 pm | | | | | | | |
| 8 pm | | | | | | | |
| 9 pm | | | | | | | |
| 10 pm | | | | | | | |
| Notes: | | | | | | | |

Here is an example of one filled out for a busy school principal.

| Name: Top Gun Principal | | | | Date: | | | |
|---|---|---|---|---|---|---|---|
| | Monday | Tuesday | Wednesday | Thursday | Friday | Saturday | Sunday |
| 5 am | | | | | | | |
| 6 am | Personal Fitness | | | | | | |
| 7 am | Quiet Time and Daily Planning and Scheduling | | | | | | **Family and Personal Time** |
| 8am | Plan with Secretary | | Principals Meeting at Central Office | | Planning Time to develop Weekly Plan | **Family and Personal Time** | |
| 9 am | Appraisals, Walkthroughs, Writeups | | | | Examine Lesson Plans | | |
| 10 am | | | | | Look at student performance data | | |
| 11 am | Return Phone Calls and Check email | | | | | | |
| Noon | | | | | | | |
| 1 pm | | | | | | | |
| 2 pm | | | | | | | |
| 3 pm | | | | | | | |
| 4 pm | | | | Staff Meeting | | | |
| 5 pm | Paperwork, return phone calls, check email | | | | | | |
| 6 pm | | | | | | | |
| 7 pm | Evening Events | Evening Events | Family and Personal Time | Evening Events | Evening Events | Possible Evening Event | |
| 8 pm | | | | | | | |
| 9 pm | | | | | | | |
| 10 pm | | | | | | | |
| Notes: | | | | | | | |

Using a time picture will assist you in budgeting time to accomplish your plans and deal with the unexpected things that occur. When an interruption occurs, having a time picture and a plan will keep the interruption from being a disruption. When our thought power is siphoned away by an interruption, we need a quick look at how to recover our focus.

Another useful tool to go along with the weekly time picture is a weekly plan. The following is an example of a weekly plan form.

| Date: |
| --- |

## ⊞ *CQL*

CENTER FOR QUALITY LEADERSHIP INC.
ACHIEVEMENT. EXCELLENCE.

# Weekly Plan

*Remember the importance of positive, excited, expectant successful mindset!*
*Check the Heat Map/Opportunity Map and Project Record*
*Organized Thought – Organized Action*
*What do you want to accomplish this week?*
*Why? What drives that purpose?*
*What am I going to do about it?*

| OBJECTIVES (What I plan to have accomplished by the end of the week) | | | |
| --- | --- | --- | --- |
| | | | |
| | | | |
| | | | |
| | | | |
| | | Time | |
| ACTIVITIES (activities required to accomplish objectives) | Priority | Needed | Day |
| | | | |
| | | | |
| | | | |
| | | | |
| | | | |
| | | | |
| | | | |
| | | | |
| | | | |
| | | | |
| | | | |

The reminders and questions at the top of the form along with the weekly time picture help you focus with flexibility. It is important to remember that you must leave some time for activity expansion and contraction and to expect unexpected occurrences. Therefore, you should not overload the objectives for accomplishment. But how do you do this? That is why developing a purpose statement, a vision statement, and a mission statement precedes the setting of goals, which precedes setting objectives, strategies, and tactics. You can do anything, but you can't do everything. Therefore, only choose the most important things. Similar time pictures and plans can be done for an annual plan, a monthly plan, and a daily plan of activities. These all give you a perspective and guidance to make the most of your time for accomplishing what you want to do. These assist you in organizing your thoughts to organize your actions for optimum accomplishment. Planning and execution require disciplined thought habits, but the benefits are huge and set you apart from most people.

There are many planning tools and decision-making tools to guide and assist you in your planning. All of this is putting into action the powerful thoughts and ideas that you imagine. If you only use a priority heat map, a time picture, and a weekly plan, you will be ahead of the game. Using additional tools will take your performance to next levels.

Now that you have a review of time and time pictures, consider which day of the week you want to do each thing. Many agree that the most promising day of the week for productivity is Tuesday. Monday is a good time for internal meetings and a review of the plans you have created. Tuesday should be reserved for your projects as your weekly energy is likely the most focused and strong. Wednesday and Thursday could be for meetings and continued project work. Friday is catch up, wrap up, and planning for next week. Some may also work on Saturday, but typically with a carefully planned and executed work time, we can focus on the important thing before it becomes urgent. This practice will take anyone to new heights. Not everyone is able to work the 100-hour workweek of a person like

Elon Musk! Daymond John, author of the book *Rise and Grind* also recognizes the importance of focused work time and the equally important time to rest, reflect, and renew.[9]

Discipline is what it takes to plan well and to work well. Once you have planned and established time periods for productivity, quickly making decisions to proceed is important. Inertia is an important thing to remember in productivity. Isaac Newton, a renowned mathematician and physicist, developed the law of motion. Newton built upon the concept of motion espoused by Galileo Galilei famous for his contribution to the science of motion. Inertia basically means a body at rest tends to remain at rest until acted upon by an outside force. Likewise, a body in motion tends to remain in motion until acted upon by an outside force.

Since we know neural pathways can be strengthened, it is important to have daily affirmations that we repeat to strengthen our thought inertia in motion at the time. Thoughts are things. Therefore, to strengthen the inertia of your thoughts, you should be prepared to act when you get a stimulus to do something, whether it is something good or not. By that I mean to remember to breathe, give yourself a few seconds to count down (perhaps a five-second countdown), change your behavior, change or reaffirm your mind, remove doubt and fear, and think positively. Build your momentum by thinking about what purpose, vision, mission, and goals are most important to you. Use your brain power to think, and act to overcome an improper stimulus or to get moving with your own trigger of thoughts to build your momentum for what is good. Chapter 8 goes into greater detail about exercising your will to achieve what you want most.

## Black Swan

I have previously mentioned interruptions and disruptions. Even the most thoughtful and well-planned weeks can be thwarted. There is an old saying that says, "The best laid plans of mice and men oft'times go astray." We must expect the unexpected. The black swan theory of events is that there are those events that come as a surprise, have a major impact, and are often inappropriately rationalized after the fact with the benefit of hindsight. Nassim Nicholas Taleb, a mathematician and statistician, developed the black swan theory. According to this theory, a black swan event is a highly improbable event that is unpredictable, carries massive impact, and after the fact goes beyond our ability to predict that it would occur and rationalize why we missed it. What does a Power Thinker do when a black swan event occurs? Consider conducting a scenario analysis. A scenario analysis is a process of examining and evaluating possible events or scenarios that could take place in the future and predicting the various feasible results or possible outcomes. Then one must consider the base-case scenario, worst-case scenario, and best-case scenario. To do this, begin by listing assumptions for each scenario. Next, detail all parts of each assumption. Match these details with each of the three scenarios from base to worst to best. Analyze each with convergent, divergent, and lateral thinking to get a 360-degree viewpoint. Then apply second-level thinking by asking the question, "And then what?"

## Gray Rhino

Another valuable insight is the concept of the "gray rhino," which is a combination of the elephant in the room and the improbable unforeseeable black swan. A "gray rhino" is a highly probable, high impact, yet neglected threat kin to both the elephant in the room and a black swan. Gray rhinos are not random surprises but occur after a series of warnings and visible evidence. Michele Wucker in her book *The Gray Rhino* explains how to recognize and act on the obvious dangers we ignore. It is being debated as to whether the COVID 19 pandemic of 2020 was a black swan or a gray rhino. The key difference between the two is the evidence of warning signs. Power Thinkers are mindful and alert and look for signs that may be one-off data or that form a pattern to which a probability may be considered. They may not be top of mind, but they are also not back of mind. "Eternal vigilance is the price of freedom." A Power Thinker is always alert and mindful of what is going on around them and spends some dedicated time to recognize, relate, and assimilate things that may impact them and what they are trying to accomplish. They are diligent to observe and record things for deeper reflection and study. They also look for patterns to discover possible threats.

**Pivot Point**

So, how does a Power Thinker handle the black swan and or a gray rhino, and how does that relate to planning and knowing exactly how to accomplish what you want? Power Thinkers think deeply and skillfully to establish their purpose, create their vision, develop a mission, and set goals to accomplish what they want. After this, they consider strategies and tactics to achieve what they want. While doing so, they consider multiple scenario plans. If plan A does not work, then plan B or even plan C may be the answer. In other words, they play what amounts to war games in advance so that when a black swan or gray rhino event occurs, it does not paralyze their thinking. They employ box breathing, exercise an OODA Loop, reflect on where they are now, and create a pivot point almost instantaneously with the speed of thought. They have overcome surprise and fear and control their thoughts, instincts, and intuition based upon previously considered scenarios.

Power Thinkers study the nature of potential conflicts. They unlock possibilities in their brains by staying keenly aware of new possibilities and intense activity from new paradigm carriers as they affect existing practices and products. They explore all possibilities and probabilities of new technologies and their impact. When the turning point is identified, they use creativity in their thinking and scenarios to deploy the need for a new paradigm. They essentially think about disrupting their own company or goals and situations first. They create a short list of scenarios that could be threats; they pay attention to new technologies, demographic shifts, and social trends. They consider new scenarios and models. They consider their current strengths, weaknesses, opportunities, and threats as they reflect upon how they intend to do things and how they may alter those intentions. They examine their current mindsets and consider what they would, could, and should do to set their minds in a new direction. They put themselves in the mind of the disruptors as to motives and strategies. In other words, like in a war game, they consider what the enemy is thinking. Then much like the rebirth of the phoenix from its ashes, they examine what mindset shift would be required to shift from destruction to rebirth. A great problem solver was Russell Ackoff. In his book *The Art of Problem Solving,* he asked serious thinkers the question, "What if when you woke up in the morning and it all went away last night, what would you do?".

Power Thinkers who consider the pivot points are prepared, adaptable, and collaborative with their team or mastermind alliance to develop skills of resilience. They ask the big questions that consider game-changing opportunities, emerging unmet needs, and consider how to act accordingly.

After having completed the thought experiments just described, Power Thinkers then consider their annual time picture and major things to accomplish, consider what month of the year to do certain things, develop the weekly plans and daily activities to fulfill their purpose, go on the journey of their vision, and use the vehicle of their mission to achieve their goals while adjusting their strategies and tactics as necessary because they have unlocked their brains to discover the unknown.

---

### Chapter 7 Summary:
### Powerful Planning Tools to Organize Thought for
### Accomplishment

THOUGHTS HAVE POWER. Think power thoughts. What exactly is a power thought? First, realize that where our thoughts are, we will be. Or where our thoughts go, we will go. This is why it is critical to stay away from negative or fearful thoughts and concentrate on positive and confident thoughts. Remember to renew your mind's eye daily with your written purpose, vision, mission, goals, strategies, and tactics that are based upon deep thinking and the detailed steps that you have engineered. Even though you or your team and mastermind group have formulated them, it is very important to review them daily. This helps you retain in your working memory the detail that you spent so much time to craft. Every airline pilot regardless of how many hours of experience they have, reviews a written checklist before every flight. Be part of the small number of thinkers that is in the Thomas Edison quote at the beginning of Chapter 5, "Five percent of the people think; ten percent of the people think they think; and the other eighty-five percent would rather die than think." Resist being part of the larger percent who merely think they think, and most certainly avoid being part of the huge percent who would rather die than think. Exercise power thinking for power living. Engage in a "thinkercise" to create a "thinkersized" result.

## Characteristics of a Power Thinker

Remember, Power Thinkers and thought leaders determine the quality of their thoughts to determine the quality of their actions and the quality of their lives.

## Set Your Heart and Set Your Mind

When you set your heart on something, you desperately want it. You are determined to get it. Desire trumps mere participation every time. Half-hearted participation will rarely lead to anything of value. It's like having one foot in a boat while keeping the other foot on the dock. Half-hearted devotion usually ends up in failure or only a meager accomplishment compared to whole-hearted devotion and commitment. In the next chapter, we see that will is master of mind and mind is master of the body. Will is formed once the heart is set. Once the heart is set, the mind can be set.

## Thought Leadership Principles

The quality of your thoughts determines the quality of your actions and the quality of your life. Be a Power Thinker. This is the key difference in a negative mental attitude and a positive mental attitude and the difference in a fixed mindset and a growth mindset and the difference in mere dreamers and skillful schemers who actually develop a large-scale systematic plan or arrangement for attaining a particular object or putting a particular idea into effect.

## Planning and Organized Thought with Time Pictures

We have reviewed some of the tools available to guide your thinking and assist you with your daily thought list like the airline pilots flight checklist. There are other tools available to put the list into action. Develop your attitudes, which are habits of thought that will propel you to success beyond your wildest dreams and beyond what average thinkers think about. Be the Power Thinker you are meant to be.

# 8

# WILLPOWER FOR POWERFUL ACTION

*If there is one thing, I have tried to do through these years, it is
to indent in the minds of the men of America the living fact that
when they give Will the reins and say "Drive!" They are
headed toward the heights.*

— DR. RUSSELL H. CONWELL, AUTHOR,
LAWYER, MINISTER, AND PHILANTHROPIST

## Heart, Mind, Body, Soul

Our body this side of death is very intricately formed by
the Creator. In our body a major and very important
organ is the brain. The brain in this physical body processes
stimuli from the five physical senses (hearing, sight, smell,
touch, and taste) as well as the sixth sense, also known as our
spiritual sense. It is this sense that frequently gives us our intuition—the ability to acquire knowledge without recourse to

conscious reasoning. Different fields use the word "intuition" in quite different ways, including but not limited to direct access to unconscious knowledge; unconscious cognition; inner sensing; inner insight to unconscious pattern-recognition; and the ability to understand something instinctively, without any need for conscious reasoning. The brain is to the body what the conscience is to the soul. The mind works in both.

In keeping with this work on Power Thinking, remember how the heart, mind, body, and spirit work together in harmony. The emotional heart is the domain of what one values, and it remembers the experiences which develop the conscience. The Mind is the processor of stimuli; the body supports a healthy brain function, and the spirit uses both the mind and the heart to exercise willpower for activity. Our spirit directs the heart, which directs the mind, which directs the body to move. This develops the conscience which guides the will, which is the engine for accomplishment. All of this is why purpose must be identified because purpose can drive will to succeed.

## Difference Between Mind and Soul

As we discussed earlier, the soul is the spiritual nature of humankind. The mind is our faculty of thinking, reasoning, and applying knowledge. It is human consciousness that starts in the brain and is manifested through our thoughts, actions, emotions, will, memories, and imagination. Our minds are where we decide how to act, what we should do, and how we should do it. Our mind invokes the conscience and our thought processes. In the physical body, the brain coordinates movements, feelings, and distinct functions of the body. You can touch the brain, but you cannot touch the mind. The brain is a complex physical organ that processes thought, memory, emotion, touch, motor skills, vision, breathing, temperature, hunger, and every process that regulates our body.

Our soul houses the mind and decides how we behave, and this essence is an eternal part of our being. Our soul is the seat of our will and the emotions making up our heart. The desires of our heart begin in our soul. Our heart determines our will. Will governs and directs the mind. Mind thinks according to the will. Mind governs and directs the body. Volition is the willing voluntary power in action. This is shown by a trigger, a thought, an action, and a consequence.

Our conscience resides with the soul and is the memory that is housed in the physical brain and the eternal soul with the mind. Our conscience will eternally be with us both while in this physical body and in our resurrected body in eternity. Our conscience is boss of the will. Conscience describes what a person believes is right and how a person decides what is right using the mind to think about things. Our conscience is our moral muscle and memory, which helps us understand the consequences of our thoughts and our actions. The conscience evaluates our motives for action by comparing them to the value decisions we have previously made, and then the battle for will or desire to do or not to do something takes place in our mind while consulting the conscience.

The power of emotions (desire) occurs in the mind while reflecting on past action and consequence and the allure of an action based upon an emotion of desire. Your conscience is the part of the mind that tells you whether what you are doing is right or wrong. If you have a guilty conscience, you feel guilty about something because you know or realize it was wrong. If you have a clear conscience, you do not feel guilty because you know you have done nothing wrong according to your conscience. A conscience can be formed with good or evil emotions. Deciding what is right or wrong as a value is based upon thoughts and experiences that produce outcomes that conform with good or evil. In our physical brain, these thoughts occur in the cerebral cortex, which processes sensory and motor information and makes us aware of the world around us.

The will has power to concentrate energy upon a given point —focused attention. The greater the will, the greater the capacity for clarity of vision for accomplishment. The starting point of all achievement is desire. Keep this constantly in mind. Weak desires bring weak results, just as a small fire makes a small amount of heat. On the other hand, a strong obsessive desire will produce a strong result—with resolute attention given to our actions.

Faith is the belief that something can come into being even before it happens. When it occurs, that is when faith becomes sight. It becomes sight when action is taken to produce what is believed to be possible. Applied faith is necessary for accomplishment. Without faith, nothing happens. Faith without action also results in nothing happening. Applied faith combined with the clarity of a detailed plan where thoughts have been organized with clarity and implemented with thoughtful action is the basis of all great accomplishments.

## Our Six Senses

These are the six senses. We have five physical senses and one spiritual sense. We were created with our heart (seat of emotion), our mind (ability to think), our body (currently physical), and our soul (spirit). The five physical senses are sight, hearing, touch, smell, and feeling. Our sixth sense is one of spirit, which is our immortal spirit that uses our mind (intellect) and heart (emotions) to choose and to will itself to do or not do something. It is eternal, and it is who we really are.

Our heart, not the physical organ pumping blood but the emotional part of our being, is to be guarded and cultivated because it is the wellspring of life. It is with our heart that we determine our beliefs based upon experience and stimuli with what we read, see, listen to, think about, and determine what we will value. The heart is like a freeway cloverleaf where all emotions and prejudices and wisdom converge.

The heart is the seat of the conscience and moral character. The heart is also the origin of desires, affections, perceptions, thoughts, reasoning, imagination, conscience, intentions, purpose, will, and faith or belief that we can do something. Intellectually, the heart is the subconscious mind at work and is where every thought comes from and is stored for reference to beliefs that are formed for action.

The heart houses the power of will to direct the mind to action. The heart is composed of the power of will where determination and resolve are formed based upon understanding. Understanding helps determine what is believed to be right or wrong, good, or evil. Apply your heart, and observe and learn from what you see. You will be amazed at the wisdom you discover.

## Willpower

Willpower, the capacity for a single volitional act, is the power of self-direction. Volition is the willing power in action. It is the power to voluntarily decide a course of action. Volition is generated by reason (thinking) and emotion (feeling), and it represents the willing power of action (acting). The will is like an energy that can increase in quantity and develop with quality. Care should be exercised to ensure that the will is developed with absolute adherence to wise and intelligent resolutions. While this is an awesome power, it is also an awesome responsibility that comes with Power Thinking. Be aware of the logic of the physical body versus the wisdom of our soul.

Frank Channing Haddock in his book *Power of Will* writes, "development of will has no other highway than absolute adherence to wise and intelligent resolutions. The conduct of life hinges on the will, but the will depends upon the man."[1] He further indicates that there are four steps of willing:

1. The idea comes to mind that something may be done.
2. Identification in your mind of motives or reasons relating to what may be done.
3. Identification in your mind of sufficient reason for action.
4. Putting forth in your mind of volition corresponding to sufficient reasons to act.

It is the will that makes one who they are.

Next, consider that there are seven forms of the will as identified by John Howard, a British philanthropist. Persistent will is what creates habits of behavior. Static will is the reserve to hold things in place. Impelling will is a strong driving force to desire to take action and indeed to appropriately take action. Dynamic will is the action taking place. Restraining will is the exercise of control of emotions and impulses to never take action, or to take action at the appropriate time. Explosive will is triggered and strongly releases action in the moment of decision or impulse to act. And, decisive will based upon stimulus, thought, reasoning, and determination to act.

Willpower is the outgrowth of a clear definite purpose expressed through persistent action, based on personal initiative. Envious people sometimes attribute success primarily to luck. Nothing could be more wrong. A famous quote attributed to the Roman philosopher Seneca is, "Luck is what happens when preparation meets opportunity." Success occurs when you have a clearly defined purpose for your life, and you take the initiative to follow through with action. We all make mistakes from time to time, but any action is far better than doing nothing.

The following chart shows the levels of commitment in concert with the levels of desire to form and act upon our will. Notice that it starts with desire and that as our desire increases; we must consider the levels of commitment. Imagining and thinking about something may start as a wish, but unless something is tried with persisted effort, difficulties may become obstacles that block our effort and resolve. Paul J. Myer said, "Whatever we vividly imagine, ardently desire, and enthusiastically act upon must inevitably come to pass." The following chart guides the journey by measuring the levels of desire combined with the levels of commitment. When our desire becomes obsessional and we adopt an all-in level of commitment, our everyday activity continues until success is achieved. At the bottom of the chart, we see that passion creates the fuel for action, which engages our purpose persistently. Consistent daily action on the major purpose compounds over time, which eventually leads to accomplishment of that major purpose. Once we become obsessed with the major purpose, clarity of action comes to mind and makes decision-making easy, and action steps become apparent for a clear road map. This organizes our thoughts, organizes our actions, and controls our attention to detail and delivery.

Activating Will Power

| | | Will Power (Passionate Fuel for Action) | | | | |
|---|---|---|---|---|---|---|
| | Level 5 | All In | | | | |
| | Level 4 | Continue Effort | | | | |
| | Level 3 | Try | | | | |
| | Level 2 | Plan to Try | | | | |
| | Level 1 | Think About It | | | | |
| | Level of Desire | Idea | Wish | Desire | Intense Obsessional Desire | Part of Everyday Life |
| | Passion: intensity of desire to accomplish something<br>Passion creates fuel for action that is Potent, Capable, Purposeful<br>Obsession Makes the Goal Abundantly Clear | | | | | |

(Left vertical label: **Level of Commitment**)

There is power in passion. It drives and pushes you harder to achieve it because you think about it all the time and that you desperately want to do and succeed in it. This intense desire will then lead to the exercise of the power of will to succeed. Vision and mission guided by purpose develop the will.

Willpower makes us who we are. If we have a strong focused will, we can master our body. Ask any long-distance runner and they will tell you that at some point the body stops asking you to stop and allows you to run the distance you set out to run. In other words, the strong will is the master of the body. The right will commands the mind to use its abilities to accomplish things we set out to accomplish. To develop a strong will, one must first get an idea of something that may be done. One then examines the motives or reasons as to why it could or should be done. Once sufficient reason is established, you may use the power of volition that corresponds to the sufficiency of your reasons for doing it. You have the power to decide to act on your motive and voluntarily pursue your purpose. This will open your power of thought to decide what action to take with skill and swiftness with which you transform the mind's energy into visible reality. It is the will that makes us who we are. We then resolutely stoke and rekindle the fires of desire to accomplish what we "will" ourselves to do. This strong emotional state leads to establishing not only habits of thought, but also habits of action that become our gyroscope for accomplishment. By using our mind, we may train and develop our willpower. Your brain matter is your sole workshop for success. You are the architect of your own career.

Life is a struggle at every age. Strength ebbs and flows. In the athletic world a common phrase is "no pain, no gain," which means we must leave our comfort zone and gain strength through struggle. Therefore, we must embrace struggle as a fact of life and develop more strength by struggling without stress. You grow strong only when you are forced to struggle. Struggle makes you powerful. We can train ourselves in our struggle by avoiding idleness and self-indulgence. We can provide care for our family members, encourage others, keep our thoughts, words, and acts pure rather than adulterated with the wrong things. We can manage our affairs well and do good works. We must stay strong and avoid discouragement, which is designed to thwart good works. Struggle is essential to our lives and our brain. The mind grows strong through use. Learn to use the mind to control the body. Take advantage of intermittent work and rest. Perform at optimum not at maximum. There are those who say to leave it all on the field in a game, give it all that you have, sacrifice the short term for the long term, in other words, live at maximum. However, life is a journey not a game and is lived one step at a time, not one sprint at a time.

Yes, there is an easy path and there is the right path. The easy path is the one of least resistance with little immediate struggle that sets up a long-term weakness. The difficult path is usually the right path. Over time, we develop perseverance, which is the ability to do or achieve something despite our difficulties, failure, or opposition. However, struggle and suffering produce perseverance and develops our character, which gives us hope of success. Along with this perseverance, we develop endurance, the ability to withstand hardship or adversity. We must persist in our toil and strife. The highest achieving individuals are those who have struggled the most. Struggle is critical to mastery. If we are not struggling, we are not learning.

Optimum is the amount or degree of something that is most favorable to some end. It is neither minimum or maximum. Both are extremes. Some people look for these opposite poles as solutions. The truth is that over time, with a proper mindset and with determined persistent action based upon willpower, we are enabled to accomplish more over time and sustain that accomplishment. Consistency compounds and the power of compounding is greater than the power of limited maximum effort.

> *Sow a thought reap an action;*
> *sow an action, reap a habit;*
> *sow a habit, reap a character;*
> *sow a character, reap a destiny.*
>
> — RALPH WALDO
> EMERSON.

Will, like steam, must be powerful, under control, and properly directed. It is driven by the power of desire, so consider how you stoke and rekindle your powers of desire backed up with your purpose. Will is the wonderworker that builds your life structure in this world. It is the will that makes us who we are. Will is expressed through persistent action based on personal initiative and is the power of self-direction. You use skill and swiftness of will to transform the mind's energy into visible reality. It is expressed through persistent action based on personal initiative. When the will fails, the battle is lost.

There are a variety of mindsets. There are positive ones, negative ones, assertive ones, proactive ones, and expectant ones. Depending upon how you feed your mind, any mindset can be developed, and it can be transcended. A mindset is a collection of thoughts and beliefs that shapes your thought habits. A mindset is a fixed mental attitude that predetermines a person's response and interpretation of situations. Therefore, exercise caution to beware of blind spots in your thinking. Understand that your blind spots can be self-deceptive. Beware the trap of a mind drift. Yes, you must have a mind flow before you develop a mindset, but mind flow is intentional while mind drift is a path of least resistance. Therefore mindfulness, a state of active open attention to the present, can allow one to live in the present, not the past or the future, and is a tool to help awareness of your physical and emotional conditions in real time. Mindfulness encourages awareness and intention. Mindfulness is also a key element in stress reduction and overall happiness. By practicing mindfulness, you may even have a mind shift.

A shift in mindset can be caused by creating something out of a fine balance between insights and innovation leading to the mind shift. A mind shift is a change in a mindset brought about by newly discovered insights through innovative thinking and discovery. Change is constant in that it is always happening. Because of this, one must always be aware and open to examining that change due to new discovery that is reflected against fundamental truth. One may need to shift their thinking due to current and new circumstances.

Mindfulness and awareness keep one keen to changes that have occurred, are occurring, and may be about to happen. Joel Barker, in his book *Paradigms: The Business of Discovering the Future,* discusses the importance of anticipation or a way of thinking about the future.[2]

There are those who think about the content of the future and those who think about the process of the future. A quantum thinker does both simultaneously. In other words, not just the "whats" of content but also the "hows" of taking meaningful action. Knowledge without action is of little value. Knowledge with action leads to understanding and wisdom. A paradigm is a pattern or model of something. In other words, a shared set of assumptions or perceptions. Paradigms are valuable in that they provide an advantage of being able to create a valid set of expectations about what will probably happen in the world based upon a shared set of assumptions. Barker indicates that a paradigm is a set of rules and regulations that establishes and defines boundaries and tells you how to behave inside the boundaries in order to be successful. But, when the assumptions and rules change and a new game appears, there will be a paradigm shift. That shift requires Power Thinkers and thought leaders to use the power of the mind to anticipate, problem solve, avoid certain problems, and identify opportunities to survive and thrive. That then is a change to a new game, a new set of rules. Most times the new paradigm is developed by someone working outside the existing paradigm. Barker refers to them as paradigm pioneers. What is impossible today is only impossible in the context of a current paradigm. Seeing the future more clearly may mean pausing our views of the certainty of our current paradigm. We either enhance our current paradigm or we shift to a new paradigm. Power Thinkers are mindful that thought leaders keep their eyes on the horizon and observe trends that are occurring in order to challenge what may be valued as status quo to lead with a long-term perspective.

An inscription on the statue on the right of the main entrance to the National Archives of the United States reads "Eternal vigilance is the price of freedom." Price is what it costs; freedom is the value received for the cost. Power Thinkers are vigilant thinkers among other thinking traits. Power Thinkers are also paradigm pioneers who become Thought Leaders who lead between the ever-shifting paradigm transformations.

Mindset, as previously discussed, is an idea that many people use as a term without fully understanding its power. It is a known fact that people have been told to set their mind on certain things. For example, in the story of Daniel, the scriptures tell us that he set his mind to gain understanding and to humble himself before God and God took care of him in his position of power and in the traumatic experience of the lion's den.

There are countless examples throughout history where individuals set their mind to do certain things. Once a direction is set, the mind is employed to act. Depending upon the focus, it is either a fixed mindset or a growth mindset to accomplish that thing. Since the one thing that we have total control of is our thoughts, we can direct those thoughts if we choose. We can indeed set our mind on anything. It is like a mental attitude or inclination. The mindset becomes a powerful belief. James Allen wrote *As a Man Thinketh*, which basically indicated that as we think, so we become.[3] Carol Dweck in her book *Mindset: The New Psychology of Success*, indicates that there are basically two kinds of mindsets: a growth mindset and a fixed mindset.[4] This is primarily attitudinal and not a genetic established mindset. She asks questions and makes statements that, depending upon how one answers them, determines if that person has a fixed mindset or a growth mindset. The mind is powerful and whatever you believe you can achieve or whatever you think you cannot do; you cannot do until you believe that you can.

The Great Houdini, Harry Houdini from Budapest, Hungary, was a magician and an escape artist. He freed himself from jails, handcuffs, chains, ropes, and straitjackets, often while hanging from a rope in the sight of street audiences. He boasted that he could escape from any jail in the world. There was once a small town that had built a new jail and invited Houdini to come try to escape the newly built state of the art jail. He accepted the challenge. Once inside the jail, he removed his jacket where he had hidden any number of assistive devices and started to work on the lock of the jail door. After thirty minutes, he began to sweat and worked even harder to open the door. After one hour, he collapsed against the door, which opened. You see, it had never been locked except in Houdini's mind. That is why it is said that if you believe you can, you can. And if you believe you cannot, you cannot.

Which mindset do you have? What do you want to become? How do you know? Do you have faith in your ability for accomplishment? Whether you believe you can or believe you can't, you are correct. The power of faith and belief in accomplishment is just that, the power to accomplish or not accomplish what you want.

Whenever you set your mind, you seek after what you want, you become intent on getting it, you strive for it and it becomes a way of thinking and living with a constant focus and reflection of your process. You make the choice daily. Your mindset should be reviewed each day and becomes your daily bread so that you will follow through on the necessary action for accomplishment. A mindset enables one to avoid distraction and to be aware of the right possibilities. Listen to this right voice. Stand strong and keep your eyes on the prize. Stay prepared. Protect your innermost thoughts, your mind, your actions and fill your mind and heart with the right things.

Avoid doubt, keep the faith, and walk on solid ground. Focus on process rather than outcome daily, but know your definite major purpose. Imagine all the steps it will take to achieve what you want. Consider what challenges you will face and what strategies you will employ to overcome the challenges. Take control of your mind and focus on the journey first, and then on the destination. Action taken based upon values, decisions, and habits of thought will employ the reality that consistency compounds. Right actions will compound; wrong actions will compound; no action will compound until you are paralyzed. Therefore, make sure that your habits of thought, attitudes, and actions are taking you where you want to go. In other words, take righteous aim.

A mindset once determined and followed with persistence equals willpower. A powerful saying is will with righteous aim creates character. Character with righteous will creates noblest aim. Character with noblest aim creates righteous will. Motive, action, willpower equals persistence. These are the pathways to accomplish whatever you desire.

What is the difference in mindset and attitude? Your mindset is your collection of thoughts, opinions, and beliefs that shape your thought habits about a particular thing, person, or approach to thinking. An attitude is a habit of thought. Remember, habits are at first cultivated and then become automatic, giving little or no conscious thought to do something. Attitudes become a way of thinking while mindsets are a shaping of your attitudes. When you first have a thought, you begin to evaluate it against the store of knowledge and experiences and determine whether you want to further explore that thought or whether you have predetermined due to your mindset that you either cannot or will not explore further. This is based upon whether your mindset is in a fixed mode or a growth mode.

Mindset that is determined and combined with persistence equals willpower. You have been given the ability to set your mind on a higher plane and not be a drifter. Think about things that have a noble calling, which are right and pure and admirable. If you persevere in your pursuit of these things, you will be highly effective and productive and accomplish more than you or anyone else believed was possible. Thought is the soul of action and the seat of action. Select with care what you read and watch, your environment, your associates, and the amount of time that you devote to developing your mind. Don't collect garbage in your mind. Remember in the discussion of brain chemistry or neurochemistry that when you hear a question that is intriguing to you, the brain releases a hit of dopamine, the pleasure chemical and your Gamma brain waves emerge. Staying intrigued is like intellectual sparring. Before you set your mind on something, it is okay to engage in reverie or free thought, daydream, study, let yourself go into a trance like state, and use the right hemisphere of your brain and engage with Infinite Intelligence to gain imagination and ideas or hunches that you can then engage the executive section of your brain to decide a mindset.

Mindset is but one of the three "Ms" of the mind. Also consider mindfulness and movement. Hal Elrod, author of *The Miracle Morning,* said, "Focused, productive, successful mornings generate focused, productive successful days—which inevitably create a successful life—in the same way that unfocused, unproductive and mediocre mornings generate unfocused, unproductive and mediocre days, and ultimately a mediocre life."[5] You must wake up determined to have a great morning, as the first three hours of your day will set the course of your overall performance.

## Sources of Forces

Unbridled will plus bold persistence and sheer force of will is a highly focused and powerfully directed energy field in the direction of your burning desire with the clear intent of refusing any other options, accepting nothing less, but being flexible to receive it. Force of will travels through the ether, the sky, and the air above the clouds, and on into the heavens. Hence the saying, "The sky is the limit." Force of will is the ability to keep on trying despite difficulties. It involves strength and energy. The only limits are those imposed by yourself. Just realize that there are good forces and there are bad forces. Exercise care in your selection of forces by being mindful of their sources.

## Transmutation

A mutation is a significant and basic alteration. An alteration is an adjustment, change, or modification. This is a change to the basic structure. Transmutation is a process of making the change to the basic structure. In mathematics we use permutations and combinations to represent a group of objects in a set. The order of the set is important in permutations since the order of something can change its meaning. In a set of combinations, the order does not matter, only the grouping matters. An example would be a mix of various candy pieces in a bowl. Recently, my youngest grandson wanted some M&M candy from a bowl. He wanted a variety of colors to enjoy. That was a combination, not a permutation. The number of each piece and the order it fits into the bowl makes a combination in a set but not a permutation. A permutation can seem like a combination when the order of numbers constitutes a password on a device or a sequence of numbers on a touchpad to unlock something.

Transmutation is the conversion of one thing into another such as changing desired behavior into another desired behavior like lighting a match. In the thought process, this means changing behavior from unacceptable urges or feelings or stimuli by channeling the impulses to engage in a different behavior. It involves conscious thought to choose a different stimulus guided by conscience and value systems. This involves seeking mind stimulus from the sixth sense rather than the five physical senses. The sixth sense makes use of the subconscious mind and communicates within the storehouse of the subconscious mind and therefore is open to Infinite Intelligence and outside mental stimulation or through the mastermind experience and guided by conscience.

Only you have control of your thoughts. Sources of good give you thoughts to strengthen you and build you up. Sources of evil have the strategy to plant unhealthy thoughts in your mind and repeatedly put them forth hoping to establish a neural pathway to control your thoughts and make you do as they desire. Be mindful of this, and don't let those sources have free rein of your mind. Believe and trust in the source of good thoughts, and beware of the source of evil and harmful thoughts. Take every thought captive until you verify its purpose before allowing it to take traction in your mind and heart. Let a well-trained conscience become your guide. Again, good thoughts are sourced to build you up while evil and bad thoughts are sourced to take you down and keep you down with a negative mental attitude.

Genius is developed through the sixth sense with creative imagination and is cultivated and developed only through use. Therefore, set your mind on the things you genuinely want that match your values and what is right rather than setting your mind on things that are tempting but not useful. Project yourself forward and consider the future result. Imagine yourself looking back from that future and having as few regrets as possible. Imagine if you will regret this action or regret not taking this action. This removes short-term emotional turmoil and allows you to focus on what you genuinely want and remember the why (purpose) that leads you to want it. Open the eyes of your heart to remember your major definite purpose and not something that is a momentary distraction that really will not matter in the future as you look back.

Remember the following virtues: moderation in indulgence, justice, prudence, strength of mind, faith, hope, love, kindness, goodness, faithfulness, and peace. Virtue is a moral practice or action and involves moral excellence, rectitude, valor, and chastity. You can live a virtuous life by not conforming to the herd mentality but by transforming yourself with the renewing of your mind to the things that are right and good. You can do whatever you want that doesn't violate the laws of God or the rights of your fellowman.

## Transformation

Our thoughts can transform our lives. Rewiring our neural pathways by creating new thoughts and behaviors allows us to form or transform ourselves into something entirely new. This is how we unlock our brain.

Project yourself forward by considering the future and imagine looking back from that future and having as few regrets as possible. Consider that in "x" years, will you regret this action or regret not taking this action? This removes short-term emotional turmoil by keeping your mind on immediate, intermediate, and distant desirable objectives. Open your mind and learn to see the future based upon trends that you see in your thinking and in the thinking of others as the behaviors of the world continue. Develop a magnificent obsession for the accomplishment you want to make. Daily focus on your goal and daily act on that goal. Let the goal dominate your thoughts and feelings. Work long hours on this labor of love by using persistent ideas, imagination, and desire for that accomplishment. This keeps you busy and occupies your thoughts and uses your energy for accomplishment. Remember the law of the harvest, "you reap what you sow." Don't let anyone come and sow weeds in your thoughts or pull up your plants. Have the proper attitude and habits of thoughts to remain steadfast and unmovable. Remember your definite main purpose. Your main purpose is your guide, for if you don't know what you want in life, what do you think you will get? Transmutation is a powerful tool for you to know and own your own mind to transform your behavior.

## Stay Productive

Don't sacrifice creativity. While excellence is a combination of efficiency and effectiveness, a total focus on them can stifle creativity. There is a time to focus on producing excellence, but using creativity to achieve the excellence is necessary. Parkinson's law states that work expands to fill the available amount of time that is allotted. It is important to therefore allot ample time for creativity. While creativity cannot be forced, picking the right time, the right environment, and the appropriate tools to engage in creative thought is important. This is a matter of choosing presence over productivity by thinking about what is truly important in the long run.

You can schedule time to do nothing. During that time, your mind can find a rhythm juggling pieces of information to look for knowledge, understanding, and wisdom. This is not an excuse to become a lazy thinker. It is about finding an appropriate ratio of time spent in productivity as well as an appropriate amount of time spent in creative thinking. Just as it makes sense to avoid distractions while meeting an established deadline, it is also wise to avoid productivity distractions during a time for creative thinking. It means being present in the moment for the chosen activity. Set aside necessary breaks from the intensity of action. There is no set formula for this, so each person must consciously determine what ratio of work and rest is best for them. Our brain consumes energy in thought, especially when we are focused on a deadline. So, a brain break for creativity can recharge the energy it takes for productivity. Creativity feeds productivity.

Productivity is "doing," but a productive part of doing includes resting, learning, observing, and thinking. True productivity is that which leads us to great accomplishment. So, what is currently top of mind for you? What questions are you willing to think about now? Gloria Steinem once said, "Without leaps of imagination, or dreaming, we lose the excitement of possibilities. Dreaming, after all, is a form of planning."

Your mind is your workshop that transforms its energy into visible reality because of your will. Will is housed in the mind and is guided by the conscience. It has been said that the will is the soul itself exercising self-direction. However, the soul must decide how and for what purposes this power shall be exercised. We have mentioned previously the elements of willpower and volition in earlier chapters.

## Self-Control

Establishing routines to reinforce good habits and destroy bad habits. Self-control is the destruction of the desire to indulge unhealthy habits. Therefore, keep the right idea foremost in mind, either the reaching of the goal or the consequence of yielding. You become what your habits make you. Since we can establish and control our habits, we can become what we desire and believe if we act with frequency. Keep your mind on things you should and do want and off the things you shouldn't and don't want. The more you accomplish, the more you can accomplish. We act according to who we believe we are. We can capture every thought and compare it to what we honestly believe and want. We compare it to our conscience which is guided by truth and what is right. We reprogram our mind to think what is right and good. This is how we unleash our full potential and free ourselves to help others. That is why we think about what is true, honorable, just, pure, lovely, and excellent.

## Make a Change

Embrace a change of heart for powerful desire. How do we reaffirm our purpose or establish a new purpose? What do we want the most? An obsessive desire is required for accomplishment as is a change in mindset based upon a well thought purpose, vision, mission, and target goal. As stated earlier, one can have many mindsets, but each mindset process is essentially the same. How do you set your mind on something?

When a new idea appears that you would like to accomplish, study extensively about what you want to achieve and refrain from thinking about what used to consume your thoughts and desires. Read books and articles and visit with knowledgeable people about the new thing or direction you are wanting to set in your mind. Increase your learning and understanding. Do deep thinking and research. Engage in physical activity to clear your mind, get oxygen to the brain with proper breathing and activity, and begin the activity that will support your desired direction of mind. Offer to do something in that endeavor for no charge to someone who may already be doing what you want to do. This way you can learn firsthand without a huge investment in time, energy, and materials if this indeed becomes your mindset.

Next, take your mind off what you don't want or no longer want, even if they are alluring. Establish new thought habits and build a fervent desire for the new thing that you want to set your mind on to develop a mindset. Remember, consistency compounds to build or maintain habits and attitudes, so think with regularity. The Japanese word for heart and mind is "*kokoro*," which means the combination of heart and mind. *Kokoro* is the merging of the heart and mind into your actions. It involves physical, mental, and emotional training. The Navy

SEALs use *kokoro* to develop mental toughness as well as attitudes of emotional resilience. They essentially put themselves through the crucible of struggle and endurance to overcome obstacles, tame the mind, and replace fear with faith. This builds their belief in their trained ability to accomplish. Whenever we state that whatever the mind can conceive and believe it can achieve, we know that this is not a simple and shallow statement but is the active power and potential we all can have when we first set our heart (emotion) and mind (thought processor) in motion to make a change. Dedicate and devote yourself with your whole heart. In this you are completely and sincerely devoted and determined in a very sincere and deeply felt way marked by complete earnest commitment, free from all reserve or hesitation.

This requires a no-holds-barred commitment to think properly and act properly. It is a clear decision backed up with devotion of thought, emotion, time, and activity focused on the mindset. This recognizes the motivation of diligence, clearing the mind for action, removal of the fear and doubt of anything but accomplishment. This then helps in developing a burning obsessive desire to achieve. This then is when you have developed the power of will.

**Bear Fruit**

Before something can bear fruit, something must first be planted and nurtured. This has sometimes been called the Law of the Harvest. Whether the seeds are seeds of thought or agricultural seeds, the principle is the same. In this case we are referring to seeds of thoughts, which become neural pathways that can be triggered by stimuli. Stimuli in our brains work with a trigger, a thought, an action, and then a consequence. After the stimuli, the important part is the thinking part prior to action. What if in our relationships we wanted to bear the fruit of love, joy, peace, forbearance, kindness, goodness, and fidelity? What thoughts and what routines would a person need to trigger when a stimulus occurred that would challenge this fruit? If we develop our own strong triggers of thought, then we could steer our thoughts to what we wanted to do rather than to react when someone or something else triggers a stimulus. Having identified and declared your mindset you can now bear its fruit. Look for opportunities in opposition to your challenges. Use your willpower to act with zeal. Establish good roots. Good roots yield good fruit.

---

## Chapter 8 Summary:
## Willpower for Powerful Action

### Heart, Mind, Body, Soul

Understanding is based upon knowledge and is also the antecedent of wisdom. It is important to understand that we are a soul (spirit) in this temporary body that ages while we are in it. Our brain is where the mind operates in the fearfully and wonderfully created body by the Creator. Mind also operates in the eternal part of us known as the soul. Heart is the seat of our emotions. Jesus of Nazareth said, "Where your treasure is, there your heart will be also." Treasure is wealth that is stored up. Wealth is what you value. What you value and desire to value is what sets your purpose and then sets your vision and determines your mission, which leads to your goals that employ strategies and tactics to solve the problem to accomplish what you want. Heart is eternally with you both while we are in this temporary body and in our eternal spirit.

There are those who have accomplished things and have left thoughts behind that are still valuable to those who follow because of the wisdom that has been recorded. The great philosophers and inventors leave behind the fruit of their labor for others to enjoy. In that way those things continue even after they are gone. Their mind was available while in the physical body, and their mind is still with them in their eternal spiritual body. This is how the Creator made it. So, the beginning of willpower is where your heart's desire sets it. Will starts with the heart. That is why we must be careful and thoughtful about what we set our heart on as that determines our treasure, i.e., the valuable things we want to accumulate be they tangible or intangible. We were created with free will and can use that will to accomplish great things.

## Willpower in Action

Your value depends on what you know and value about yourself. Your direct and conscious development of will is the power within you. Try it, evaluate it, and if practical and useful, adopt it to unlock your brain, discover the unknown, and accomplish your best work. Be a Power Thinker, be a thought leader, and serve both yourself and others.

## Final Thought to Remember

Will is master of the mind; mind is master of the body. A master thinker can become a master mind of amazing accomplishments.

A mind master is someone who understands how the mind works and who realizes that whatever they conceive and believe they can achieve. They exercise creative vision (discovering opportunities), define their major purpose (prioritization), and develop and implement an action plan with detail (commitment). A master mind is someone who creates new things based upon deep thought and expertise and is willing to work on complex things. Exercising your power of will as a Power Thinker enables you to become a thought leader.

## Final Willpower Quote

"Strength does not come from physical capacity.
It comes from an indomitable will." —Gandhi

# EPILOGUE

King Solomon, the wise king and writer of the book of Ecclesiastes, said that he applied his mind to study and to explore by wisdom all that is done under the heavens. He applied wisdom and knowledge with understanding. He also said there is a time for everything:

## To Everything There Is a Season

To everything there is a season,
and a time for every purpose under heaven:
a time to be born and a time to die,
a time to plant and a time to uproot,
a time to kill and a time to heal,
a time to break down and a time to build,
a time to weep and a time to laugh,
a time to mourn and a time to dance,

a time to cast away stones and a time to gather
  stones together,
a time to embrace and a time to refrain from
  embracing,
a time to search and a time to count as lost,
a time to keep and a time to discard,
a time to tear and a time to mend,
a time to be silent and a time to speak,
a time to love and a time to hate,
a time for war and a time for peace.[1]

He then said that there is nothing better for a person than to enjoy their work because that is their lot. Therefore, we should invest in many ventures. What will you do in each season of your life? How will you organize your genius? How will you manage your performance? Will you apply wisdom to your knowledge and understanding? Do you realize that not everything has been discovered yet? The Wright brothers flew an airplane for the first time at Kitty Hawk on December 17, 1903. The Wright Brothers made that flight of twelve seconds in a power-driven heavier-than-air machine that changed the history of the world. Elon Musk, Richard Branson, and Jeff Bezos all dreamed of flying in space as private citizens. They did it in 2021, more than a hundred years after the invention of the airplane and after many government-led missions by multiple governments. Will they ever develop a living space on the moon or on Mars? Where do they get such imagination?

The quality of your thoughts determines the quality of your life. Tony Robbins said, "I don't negotiate with my mind, it does what I want, not the other way around."[2] This means that we can literally design our own future as Power Thinkers.

Everything is the tool of thoughts. Thoughts are things, and when powerfully mixed with a clear purpose, persistence, and a burning desire exercised with volitional will for their translation into riches or other material objects, there is no end to what you can do.

Are you ready to develop and apply your Power Thinking skills to become a thought leader in your field? Being perceived as a thought leader may be positive for your career. Your opinions and thoughts matter, and they can help move others to change points of view or to act because of your thought leadership. Your mission—should you choose to accept it—is to develop the thinking skills proven to raise your performance and professional standing to levels beyond what you currently imagine.

Have you ever wondered about where you are in life and where you could go if you let yourself go for it? I wondered if there was a way that I could become a thought leader or paid expert who could share collected wisdom. I wondered if I had anything to say that would be helpful to others. I began to believe that this was a calling that I must answer.

Invest in yourself. You deserve to develop your expertise to its highest level. You deserve to become a Power Thinker to discover the unknown by unlocking your brain. You deserve to become a foremost authority in your selected area of specialization to become the go-to individual or organization for that expertise and get paid for it.

What if you could become a Certified Thought Leader (CTL)? Would this enhance your professional standing? Thought leaders stand out.

Consider your learning plan. Never stop learning, go back to school, read books, get training, and acquire skills. Thought leaders look for wisdom and discipline their thinking. Thought leaders are wise and add to their learning. Thought leaders are discerning and seek guidance for understanding that leads to wisdom.

A thought leader is an individual or firm that is recognized as one of the foremost authorities in selected areas of specialization, resulting in being the go-to individual or organization for that expertise. Thought leadership status is achieved by expertise, insight, and a valuable perspective that is formed over time.

Thought leadership requires dedication and hard work. Thought leaders are individuals who examine the past, recognize and analyze the present, while imagining and illuminating the future. Thought leaders focus on the why before they focus on the how. Why are we doing this in the first place? Why does it matter? Thought leaders assist any organization that they are a part of as it navigates necessary change.

A thought leader has the curiosity to learn with a commitment to add to and hone their knowledge in a particular field and then willingly shares that knowledge. Thought leaders are perceived as knowledgeable sources of insight in a chosen field or subject matter area—they are experts. Simply put, a thought leader is someone other people listen to about a certain subject.

Thought leaders are humble learners. They recognize that there are people out there who know their field much more deeply than they do. Never rest on what you already know, even if you're the brightest in your field. Adopt the attitude that, in any discipline, you can never know more than 1 percent of what there is to learn. It keeps you humble and hungry.

Do you have what it takes to become a Certified Thought Leader? It takes expertise in a particular niche. It takes an ongoing involvement in (or awareness of) that niche. A clearly identified point of view. It takes credibility and a supportive following. It's a truism that thought leaders tend to be the most successful individuals.

The purpose of a thought leader is to provide people with valuable, accurate, timely information based upon deep thought and study on a consistent basis that they can believe and trust. A thought leader is dedicated to hard work and solving deep problems that require deep thought and expertise. Mind power is essential. Not everyone is dedicated to the hard work of deep thought, so thought leaders are vital to creating a better future.

That is why thought leaders observe, connect, and create ideas for their field of expertise. They create a comprehensive, unique and impactful view of an area of expertise and bring a point of view to the table that cannot be obtained elsewhere. They have answers to the biggest questions in the minds of their stakeholders. Thought leadership becomes effective when your passion and expertise coincide with the interest of your stakeholders. Thought leaders are involved in the decision-making process to gain alignment. Thought leaders see trends first. They use thinking tools to skillfully solve problems, make decisions, and lead the way for future benefits. It's tough to commit to never-ending improvement, but that's what the exceptional ones do.

You deserve to become a CTL. This is what most Power Thinkers choose to do. The courses are online through CQL Academy offered by the Center for Quality Leadership. After the first three courses, you become a Leading Thinker, the next three qualify you as a Master Thinker, the final three qualify you as a Power Thinker. Finally, after completion of a thought experiment, you qualify to be designated as a CTL, a Certified Thought Leader. Also, we conduct an annual Master Mind Vertex for thought leaders across all industries. To find out more, go to our website, www.cql.net.

**CQL**

CENTER FOR QUALITY LEADERSHIP INC.
ACHIEVEMENT. EXCELLENCE.

# ABOUT THE AUTHOR
## DON HOOPER, PH.D., CTL

**Dr. Don Hooper** is a thought leader. He is a mastermind who helps clients master their minds. With a Ph.D. in Administrative Leadership and Management, Dr. Hooper specializes in helping others turn their creative thoughts into organizational excellence and become thought leaders in their own right.

Dr. Hooper is the Executive Director at School Research Nexus and President and Founder of the Center for Quality Leadership, a business consulting firm that provides leadership management training and has transformed the lives of thousands of leaders over the past three decades. He served as a School Superintendent for over 25 years and was President of the American Association of School Administrators, President of the Texas Association of School Administrators, and Education Co-Chair of the Texas Business Education Coalition. Dr. Hooper received much recognition for his efforts in the education space and was voted Superintendent of the Year by the Texas Association of School Administrators, Educator of the Month by Texas School Business Magazine, and Member of the Business Hall of Fame for the Center for Quality Leadership Inc. by the Missouri City Award Program.

A proud father of five children, twenty grandchildren, and

seven great-grandchildren (and counting!), Dr. Hooper draws inspiration from his family every day and credits them with helping transform his life. He now continues to pay it forward through his work transforming the lives of others.

Learn more about Dr. Hooper and his work at www.cql.net.

in  linkedin.com/in/don-hooper

# NOTES

## Prologue

1. Hill, N., & Clement Stone, W. 1997. *Success Through a Positive Mental Attitude: Discover the Secret of Making your Dreams come True*. Thorsons.

## 2. Executive Stewardship: Using Mindset for Mastering Leadership

1. Wikipedia contributors. 2022. *The Four-Way Test*. Wikipedia, The Free Encyclopedia. https://en.wikipedia.org/w/index.php?title=The_Four-Way_Test&oldid=1091242004.
2. Morris, E. 2020. *Edison*. Random House Trade Paperbacks.

## 3. How to Use Your Brain for Powerful Change

1. Bennis, W. G., & Nanus, B. 1985. *Leaders: Strategies for Taking Charge*. HarperBusiness.
2. Wikipedia contributors. 2022. *OODA loop*. Wikipedia, The Free Encyclopedia. https://en.wikipedia.org/w/index.php?title=OODA_loop&oldid=1087709394.
3. Brady, T. 2020. *The TB12 Method: How to Do What You Love, Better and for Longer*. Simon & Schuster.

## 4. Using Power Thinking for Problem Identification, Prioritization, and Power Solutions

1. PeriodBuddy. 2019. "Short Stories that Will Change the Way You Think-MARC CHERNOFF, *The Weight of the Glass*." PeriodBuddy. June 3, 2019. https://periodbuddy.care/short-story-the-weight-of-the-glass.
2. Ziglar, Z. 2015. "Your Altitude." Ziglar Inc. https://www.ziglar.com/quotes/your-attitude-not-your-aptitude/.
3. Toffler, A. 1970. *Future Shock*. Bodley Head.

4. Scialabba, G. 1984 "The Browser: Mindplay." *Harvard Magazine*, Volume 86, Number 4, March-April 1984.
5. Guilford, J.P. 1967. *The Nature of Human Intelligence*. Mcgraw-Hill.
6. Edwards Deming, W. (1988). *Out of the Crisis (2nd ed.)*. Cambridge University Press.
7. Ibid.

## 5. Power Thinking Tools for Power Leadership

1. Ecclesiastes 1:17.

## 6. Finding Your Power Purpose

1. Covey, S. R. 2013. *The 7 Habits of Highly Effective People: Powerful Lessons in Personal Change (25th ed.)*. Simon & Schuster.
2. Boss, J. 2019. "10 Inspirational Quotes from Navy SEAL Training." *Entrepreneur*. May 15, 2019. https://www.entrepreneur.com/slideshow/232209.

## 7. Powerful Planning Tools to Organize Thought for Accomplishment

1. Covey, S. R. 2013. *The 7 Habits of Highly Effective People: Powerful Lessons in Personal Change (25th ed.)*. Simon & Schuster.
2. Meyer, P.J. 2001. "Awards & Recognition." *IEEE Power Engineering Review, 21*(11), 64-a-64-a. https://doi.org/10.1109/mper.2001.4311195.
3. O'Leary, K. 2011. *Cold Hard Truth: On Business, Money & Life*. Doubleday Canada.
4. Easter, M. 2021. "To achieve a goal, turn it into a problem." *Forge*. February 8, 2021. https://forge.medium.com/its-better-to-solve-a-problem-than-achieve-a-goal-41799dbb9d0b.
5. Hill, N. 2016. *Think and Grow Rich: The Original, an Official Publication of the Napoleon Hill Foundation*. Sound Wisdom.
6. Hill, N. 2017. *How to Own Your Own Mind*. Tarcherperigee.
7. Porter, E. 1999. *Pollyanna*. HarperCollins.
8. Parkinson, C. N. 1955. "Parkinson's Law." *The Economist*. November 19, 1955. London, England. https://www.economist.com/news/1955/11/19/parkinsons-law.

9. John, D. 2018. *Rise and Grind: Outperform, Outwork, and Outhustle Your Way to a More Successful and Rewarding Life.* Currency.

## 8. Willpower for Powerful Action

1. Haddock, F. C. 2015. *Power of Will: A Practical Companion-Book for Enfoldment of Selfhood Through Direct Personal Culture.* Sagwan Press.
2. Barker, J. A. 1993. *Paradigms: The Business of Discovering the Future.* HarperBusiness.
3. Allen, J. 2021. *As a Man Thinketh.* Peter Pauper Press.
4. Dweck, C. 2007. *Psychology: The New Psychology of Success.* Ballantine Books.
5. Elrod, H. 2018. *The Miracle Morning: The 6 Habits That Will Transform Your Life Before 8AM.* Teach Yourself.

## Epilogue

1. Ecclesiastes 3:1-8.
2. Pietrzak, M. 2020. May 26). Why Focusing on Your Personal Growth Now is More Important Than Ever. *SUCCESS.* May 26, 2020. https://www.success.com/why-focusing-on-your-personal-growth-now-is-more-important-than-ever/.

www.ingramcontent.com/pod-product-compliance
Lightning Source LLC
Chambersburg PA
CBHW070108030426
42335CB00016B/2067